Pediatric Round Table: 7

Sponsored by
Johnson & Johnson
BABY PRODUCTS COMPANY

Minimizing High-Risk Parenting

A Review of What Is Known and Consideration of Appropriate Preventive Intervention

Edited by Valerie J. Sasserath, Ph.D.
Introduction by Robert A. Hoekelman, M.D.

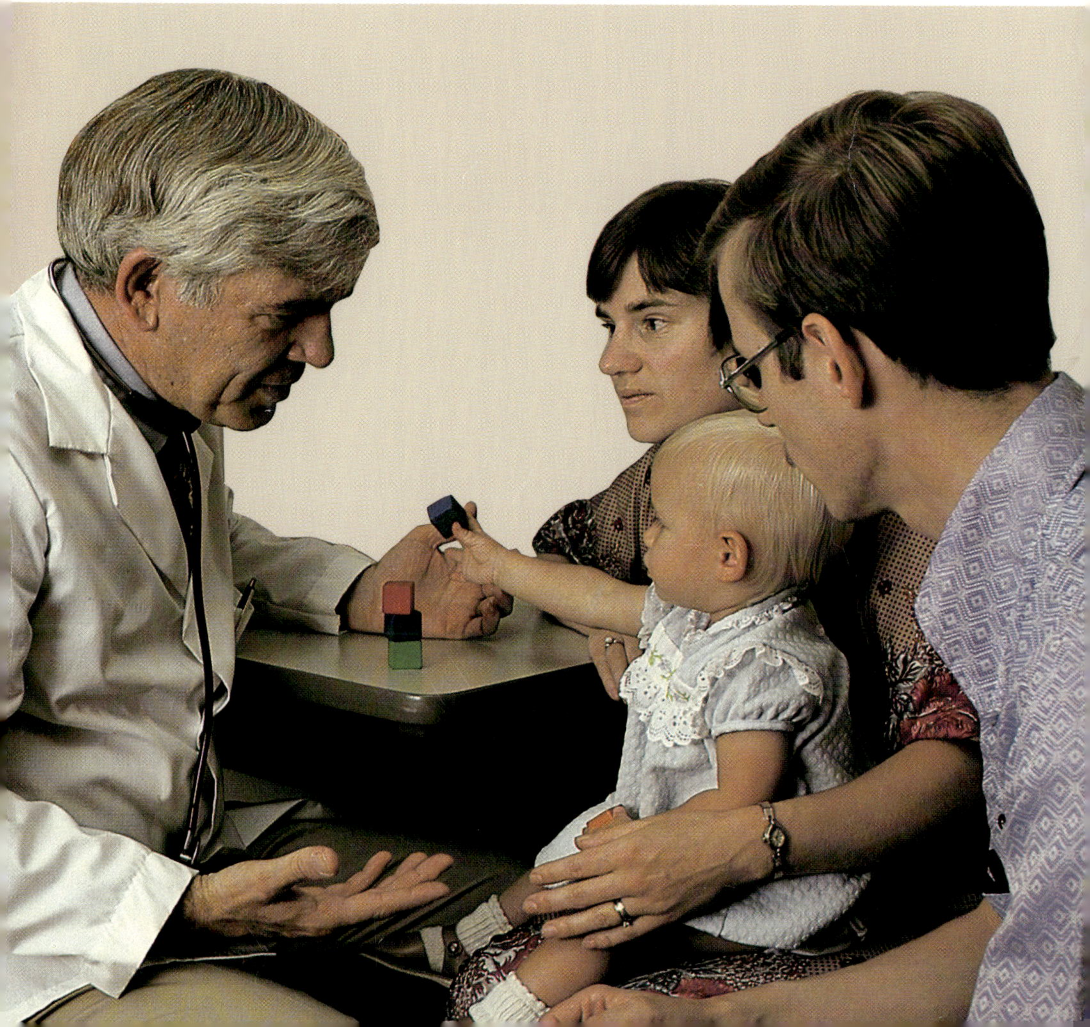

MINIMIZING
HIGH-RISK
PARENTING

Summary Publications in the Johnson & Johnson Baby Products Company Pediatric Round Table Series:

1. *Maternal Attachment and Mothering Disorders: A Round Table*
   Edited by Marshall H. Klaus, M.D., Treville Leger, and Mary Anne Trause, Ph.D.

2. *Social Responsiveness of Infants*
   Edited by Evelyn B. Thoman, Ph.D., and Sharland Trotter

3. *Learning Through Play*
   By Paul Chance, Ph.D.

4. *The Communication Game*
   Edited by Abigail Peterson Reilly, Ph.D.

5. *Infants At Risk: Assessment and Intervention*
   Edited by Catherine Caldwell Brown

6. *Birth, Interaction and Attachment*
   Edited by Marshall Klaus, M.D., and Martha Oschrin Robertson

7. *Minimizing High-Risk Parenting*
   Edited by Valerie J. Sasserath, Ph.D.

Cover: *Robert A. Hoekelman provides counseling to parents.*

Cover Photo: *Royal L. Chamberlain*

MINIMIZING HIGH-RISK PARENTING

A Review of What Is Known and
Consideration of Appropriate
Preventive Intervention

Edited by
Valerie J. Sasserath, Ph.D.

Introduction by
Robert A. Hoekelman, M.D.

Sponsored by

Johnson & Johnson
BABY PRODUCTS COMPANY

Library of Congress Cataloging in Publication Data
Main entry under title:

Minimizing high risk parenting.

  (Johnson & Johnson Baby Products Company pediatric round table; 7)

Bibliography: P.
  1. Infant psychiatry. 2. Parenting. 3. Parent and child. I. Sasserath, Valerie. II. Hoekelman, Robert A. III. Series. [DNLM: 1. Child development disorders — Congresses. 2. Parent-child relations — Congresses. WS 105.5F2 M665 1981] RJ502.5.M56 1982   616.85'82   82-14852

ISBN 0-931562-07-4

Senior Editor: *Jane Edwards*
Project Editor: *Barbara Holland*
Designer: *Louise Snyder*
Composition: *Brenda Slabaugh, June Sangiorgio*
Layout: *Eleanor D. Loflin*
Production and Manufacturing: *Cale—Prince Communications, Inc., an affiliate of Harwal Publishing*

Copyright © 1983 by Johnson & Johnson Baby Products Company

Printed in the United States of America. All rights reserved. Except as permitted under the Copyright Act of 1976, no part of this publication may be reproduced or distributed in any form or by any means or stored in a data base or retrieval system, without the prior written permission of the publisher.

1   2   3   4   5   6   7   8   9   10

For child health care professionals and parents everywhere

CONTENTS

List of Participants	ix
Preface	xi
Introduction	
Robert A. Hoekelman	xiii

PART I—SUCCESSFUL PARENTING

Introduction
   Robert A. Hoekelman, M.D.   1
Basic Adaptations Required for Successful Parenting
   Stella Chess, M.D.   5
Successful Parenting in the Black Community
   Carol Ann Leal, M.D.   11
Factors in Predicting Successful Parenting
   Arnold J. Sameroff, Ph.D.   16
Summary Comments
   Robert Bradley, Ph.D.   25

PART II—HIGH-RISK PARENTING

Introduction
   Robert A. Hoekelman, M.D.   31
Coping with Pregnancy and Parenthood
   Howard J. Osofsky, M.D., Ph.D.   33
The Vulnerable Dyad—Adolescent Mothers and Their Infants
   Elizabeth R. McAnarney, M.D.   39
Growing Hand in Hand: Infants and Parents at Risk
   Vivian Shapiro, M.S.W.   44

Parents of Medically Impaired Infants
Carolyn R. Aradine, R.N., Ph.D.   50
Parents Who Have Lost a Child by Death
Sherry Johnson-Soderberg, R.N., Ph.D.   55
Parents of the Premature Infant
Suzanne Hall Johnson, R.N., M.N.   61
When the Injury is a Symptom: Interrelations among the Pediatric Social Illnesses
Eli H. Newberger, M.D.   65
Stages of Parental Understanding in Child Abuse and Neglect
Carolyn Moore Newberger, Ed.D.   69
Interaction of Multiple Factors Contributing to High-Risk Parenting
Henry N. Ricciuti, Ph.D.   75
Parenting in Infancy and Early Childhood: A Developmental Structuralist Approach to Detailing Adaptive and Maladaptive Patterns
Stanley I. Greenspan, M.D.   79
Summary Comments
Stanley I. Greenspan, M.D.   87

PART III—PREVENTION OF HIGH-RISK PARENTING OUTCOMES

Introduction
Robert A. Hoekelman, M.D.   91
An Intervention Program For High-Risk Families
David L. Olds, Ph.D.   93
Perinatal Coaching: A Primary Prevention Model
Leslie Hoover, R.N., M.A.   99
Summary Comments
Robert A. Hoekelman, M.D.   105

APPENDIX—Funding for Cost-Benefit Analysis of Services for High-Risk Families and Infants
Nancy T. Greenspan, M.A.   109
Bibliography   113

PARTICIPANTS

Caroline Aradine, R.N., Ph.D.
Associate Professor of Nursing
University of Rochester School of
 Nursing
Chief, Clinical Pediatric Nursing and
 Nursing Practice
Strong Memorial Hospital
Rochester, New York 14642

Robert Bradley, Ph.D.
Professor of Educational Foundations
University of Arkansas
Chairman, Center for Child
 Development and Education
Little Rock, Arkansas 72204

Stella Chess, M.D.
Professor of Child Psychiatry
New York University School of
 Medicine
New York, New York 10016

James T. Dettre
Director, Marketing Services
Johnson & Johnson Baby Products
 Company
Skillman, New Jersey 08558

Nancy T. Greenspan, M.A.
Chief, Economic and Long-Range
 Studies Branch
Department of Health and Human
 Services
Office of Research
Washington, D.C. 20201

Stanley I. Greenspan, M.D.
Clinical Professor of Psychiatry and
 Behavioral Sciences and Child
 Health and Development
George Washington University
 Medical School
Washington, D.C. 20037
Chief, Clinical Infant Development
 Unit
Laboratory of Psychology and
 Psychopathology
National Institutes of Health
Adelphi, Maryland 20783

Robert A. Hoekelman, M.D.
Professor and Associate Chairman
Department of Pediatrics
University of Rochester School of
 Medicine and Dentistry
Rochester, New York 14642

Leslie Hoover, R.N., M.A.
Maternal-Child Health Nurse
 Consultant
Michigan Department of Health
Lansing, Michigan 48909

Darlene Jelinek, R.N., F.N.P.
Project Director, National Task Force
 on Family Nurse Practitioner
 Curriculum and Evaluation
Department of Family, Community,
 and Emergency Medicine
University of New Mexico School of
 Medicine
Albuquerque, New Mexico 87131

Suzanne Hall Johnson, R.N., M.N.
Neonatal Clinical Nurse Specialist
Director, Health Update
Editor, *Dimensions of Critical-Care
 Nursing*
Lakewood, Colorado 80226

**Sherry Johnson-Soderberg, R.N.,
 Ph.D.**
Assistant Professor of Nursing
University of Illinois College of
 Nursing
Rockford, Illinois 61101

Carol Ann Leal, M.D.
Assistant Clinical Professor of
 Psychiatry
Columbia University College of
 Physicians and Surgeons
Chief, Child and Adolescent
 Psychiatry
Harlem Hospital Center
New York, New York 10603

Elizabeth R. McAnarney, M.D.
George Washington Goler Associate
 Professor of Pediatrics
Director, Division of Biosocial
 Pediatrics and Adolescent
 Medicine
University of Rochester School of
 Medicine and Dentistry
Rochester, New York 14642

Carolyn Moore Newberger, Ed.D.
Instructor in Psychology
Department of Psychiatry
Harvard Medical School
Staff Psychologist
Judge Baker Guidance Clinic
Boston, Massachusetts 02115

Eli H. Newberger, M.D.
Director, Family Development Study
Children's Hospital Medical Center
Boston, Massachusetts 02115

David L. Olds, Ph.D.
Director, Prenatal/Early Infancy
 Project
Comprehensive Interdisciplinary
 Developmental Services
Elmira, New York 14901

Howard J. Osofsky, M.D., Ph.D.
Staff Psychiatrist
Menninger Foundation
University of Kansas Medical School
Topeka, Kansas 66601

Harriet Presser, Ph.D.
Professor of Sociology
University of Maryland
College Park, Maryland 20740

Henry N. Ricciuti, Ph.D.
Professor of Human Development
 and Family Studies
New York State College of Human
 Ecology
Cornell University
Ithaca, New York 14830

Robert B. Rock, Jr., M.A., M.P.A.
Director, Professional Relations
Johnson & Johnson Baby Products
 Company
Skillman, New Jersey 08558

Arnold J. Sameroff, Ph.D.
Professor of Psychology
University of Illinois
Associate Director, Illinois Institute
 for Development Disabilities
Chicago, Illinois 60608

Valerie Sasserath, Ph.D.
Science Writer
271 Varsity Avenue
Princeton, New Jersey 08540

Vivian Shapiro, M.S.W.
Senior Social Worker
Child Development Project
Department of Psychiatry
University of Michigan
Ann Arbor, Michigan 48109

Sydney A. Sutherland, M.A.
Senior Technical Associate
University of Rochester
Rochester, New York 14642

PREFACE

As the result of discussions coming out of the Johnson & Johnson Baby Products Company Pediatric Round Table #5, "Infants at Risk: Assessment and Intervention," two subjects emerged as worthy of future Round Table consideration. The first, and more immediate, is concerned with the child at risk in terms of how the many interventions associated with the parenting process can be more effectively managed to contribute to more successful outcomes. The second is an increasing recognition of the need for more effective communication between child-health professionals and parents. We felt that it would be logical to consider these subjects in this order, particularly since the Round Table on "Minimizing High-Risk Parenting" represents an immediate sequal to that on "Infants At Risk." The outcome of this decision is expressed in this summary publication, *Minimizing High-Risk Parenting*.

The Round Table proceedings, as effectively summarized by science writer Dr. Valerie Sasserath, offer child-health professionals and parents a valuable resource that represents both a consolidation of current information on the subject and a guide to interventions for situations in which high-risk parenting may occur.

Round Table participants under Moderator, Dr. Robert A. Hoekelman, Professor and Associate Chairman, Department of Pediatrics, The University of Rochester School of Medicine and Dentistry, defined high-risk parenting as a social condition in which the normal patterns of child behavior and interaction are disturbed as the result of adverse demographic or environmental situations or unique physical or socioemotional conditions. From a multidisciplinary point of view, the participants compared successful normal parenting with what is known about high-risk parenting, in terms of prevention and positive outcomes. Considerable emphasis was placed on the need to test intervention strategies, which in turn can be translated into successful outcomes, on the need to correct misconceptions and misinterpretations and, because of the enormous amount of time required for implementation, on the need for patience and effective communication. We are most grateful to the nineteen nationally acknowledged experts for their contributions. They provide a fascinating insight into the understanding of what can go wrong, how parents and their children can be adversely affected, and how child-health professionals can intervene appropriately to prevent and manage high-risk parenting situations.

Robert B. Rock, Jr., M.A., M.P.A.
Director of Professional Relations

INTRODUCTION

The objectives for the conference reported in this volume were to define the circumstances in which normal and high-risk parenting usually occur, to review current research on high-risk parenting and identify areas for future research, and to make recommendations regarding appropriate interventions that health professionals can apply to situations in which high-risk parenting may occur.

We defined high-risk parenting as a social condition in which the normal patterns of parent and child behavior and interaction are disturbed. This can be a result of adverse demographic and environmental situations or of physical, personal, or interpersonal characteristics that result in sociopathic outcomes. Normal parenting, of course, was defined as that which occurred under circumstances excluded by the definition of high-risk parenting—favorable demographic and environmental situations and ordinary physical, personal, and interpersonal characteristics for the parents and their child.

We decided on a format for presentation of the knowledge base pertaining to the subject of high-risk parenting—in this case, what is known about successful parenting, what is known about high-risk parenting, and what is known about prevention of high-risk parenting and its outcomes. This seemed a logical means for conducting an orderly discussion that would lead to a full understanding of the origins of abnormal parenting and to recommendations for successful interventions to reduce the occurrence and improve the outcome of abnormal or high-risk parenting.

We chose to begin by establishing the basis for normal parenting, so that this model could serve as the yardstick by which to measure the degree of abnormal parenting in the families we serve. In doing so, it is important to be aware that the definitions of normal parenting were derived from not only various theories but also from our own personal and professional perspectives of parenting that usually lead to good, nonsociopathic outcomes. These perspectives, based upon our experiences and those of others, are not always accurately predictive, so we must allow for some latitude in our assumptions that the absence of certain demographic, environmental, and personal predictors of normal parenting will actually result in poor parenting.

Nevertheless, it is important to explore our understanding of normal parenting outcomes, particularly the theories that govern our judgments of its factors. We were fortunate to have four people who have studied the antecedents of individual development to address the issue of successful parenting. Each has a different view of which variables are most important to individual development and normal parenting, but fortunately none is contradictory. The information they presented enabled us to move on to a discussion of high-risk parenting, well grounded in our understanding of normal parenting.

High-risk parenting stems from an infinite variety of circumstances. It is essential to define these so that parents who are at risk for dysfunctional parenting can be identified and given the assistance and support they need. In so doing, many, if not all, of the consequences of their difficulties can be successfully avoided or rectified. It is also important to recognize that the predictors of high-risk parenting do not necessarily lead to poor outcomes. Humans, fortunately, are adaptive and able to cope successfully with most of the circumstances that occasion parenting difficulties.

Our understanding of high-risk parenting derives from studies of dysfunctional parents and the application of this information to the theoretical constructs of parental development. By studying the circumstances in which things have gone wrong, we are able to determine, using a developmental framework, why they did. Thus, we are able to understand why becoming a parent for the first time can be risky and why older parents, stepparents, adolescent parents, psychologically impaired parents, isolated parents, and indigent parents are at risk. Similarly, we understand why parents of premature or medically impaired infants and parents who have lost an infant have significant problems in assuming their current and subsequent parenting roles.

Each of these situations affects parents psychologically and physically and has lasting effects on their relationships with each other and with their families and friends. The situation may generate a sense of loss or a sense of guilt, grief, anger, frustration, and exhaustion. It is not surprising, then, that we see so many parents and children suffering the consequences of childbearing and childrearing. Understanding what can go wrong and how parents and their children can be adversely affected will help us to intervene appropriately to prevent and manage high-risk parenting situations.

How long should we continue to define through research the determinants of high-risk parenting? Although making such definitions can help us plan successful interventions, we must also test intervention strategies. We must get on with that task and see whether or not what we have learned from our research—the definitions, the predictors of high-risk parenting, and the identification of high-risk individuals—can be translated into effective interventions. It is important to test those intervention strategies to see whether they are successful. We have to keep in mind that the recommendations that evolve from research take an enormous amount of time in implementation. It is also time-consuming to correct misconceptions and the misinterpretations of research data. This has been a particular problem with the issue of early attachment and bonding. It will take the public a long time to appreciate that instant bonding is not necessarily essential to successful parenting. Nevertheless, we must correct this and other misconceptions and determine what constitutes appropriate interventions in preventing and correcting high-risk parenting situations and get on with the job.

One always needs to question whether or not the objectives of any activity have been successfully achieved. This round table, I believe, attained our first two objectives fully: we were able to define the circumstances in which normal and high-risk parenting usually occur, and we were able to review current research on high-risk parenting to identify areas for future research. This identification of areas for future research seems always to be an outcome of discussions on problems such as high-risk parenting that are so prevalent and of such various cause. While we did not formally define recommendations regarding appropriate interventions that health professionals can apply to potential and actual high-risk situations—our third objective—the reader will find throughout each presentation many concrete suggestions for such interventions. He or she must decide which of these is reasonable and practical, given available resources.

This last point, is the one that I, personally, think is most important. Taking into account all that we do know about normal parenting (and its attendant risks) and about the antecedents and circumstances of high-risk parenting, there are many things we can do professionally and personally to help our patients and their friends and relatives through the difficulties of parenthood. In the larger sense, that is, in the broad application of the principles of prevention and management of high-risk parenting situations through community-based intervention programs, the prospects for success, even when we are sure of the methods, are not bright. The scope of the problem is immense, and the resources currently available to help those parents at risk are limited; in today's political atmosphere, in fact, they are diminishing. Thus, we must individually and collectively, working in both our professional and political arenas, direct our energies toward generating more resources to these ends.

Robert A. Hoekelman, M.D.

PART I
SUCCESSFUL PARENTING

The presentations in Part I address the complex issues surrounding successful parenting and focus on conceptual models of parenting, explaining their antecedents, ingredients, and consequences for child development.

According to Stella Chess, an individual's developmental outcome has roots in many antecedents, parenting being only one. Rather than rigidly defining successful parenting, Chess proposes her "goodness-of-fit" model, in which successful parenting is defined as achievement of the best possible fit between the capacities of the child and the demands and expectations of his caretaking environment. This flexible parenting model taps the maximum capacity of the child without stressing the system in which he is raised. Parents must adapt to, among other things, their child's temperament.

Carol Leal's analysis of successful parenting in the black community underscores the importance of social variables such as history, politics, culture, and economics and how parents deal with these societal forces. Leal believes that to provide children with ways to develop self-esteem and creative channels for self-gratification (two ingredients of successful parenting), black parents must first acknowledge the existence of negative stereotypes and then combat them, often within the extended family, through positive interactions with their children.

Arnold Sameroff views developmental outcome as resulting from the dynamic interplay of constitutional and environmental variables. Successful parenting, in interaction with other factors, contributes to a child's development over time. One important set of underlying variables that Sameroff is currently studying includes parental concepts of development, which vary along a continuum from concrete to abstract and which have been categorized as symbiotic, categorical, compensative, and perspectivistic.* These categories correspond to Piaget's four stages of intellectual development in children: sensorimotor, preoperational, concrete operational, and formal operational. His data indicate that the level of parental conception of development may relate to socioeconomic status, which seems to account for developmental outcome to a greater degree than any other single variable. The model proposed by Sameroff is a *transactional* model of development, which takes the *interactional* model one step further by adding the dimension of time.

These three points of view are summarized by Robert Bradley, who presents the results of his own research concerning the effects of early maternal behavior on the intellectual and behavioral development of children. According to Bradley, the three essential points made by the presenters are: (1) Linear models of parenting and child development are obsolete; we need to conceptualize and study multifaceted models that more realistically depict the course of development and the role of parenting in that process. (2) The effects of early mothering are important but not crucial in determining developmental outcomes; the impact of a variety of later experiences may be as important. Focusing on early mother-child interactions may produce high levels of guilt and anxiety in parents, which can adversely affect their parenting behaviors. (3) We must examine broader contexts when studying psychological development, because the course of human development is also affected by culture, politics, economics, and other external factors.

The points made by the presenters concerning the need to look beyond the effects of early mothering and to include the wider social and cultural contexts when examining parenting and child development are related to the abandonment of linear models. Chess believes that the Freudian and behavioral "blame-the-mother" ideologies have given way to the current bonding and attachment

---

* The ability to view situations from a variety of perspectives.

"blame-the-mother" ideologies, which she labels "mal de mère I" and the "mal de mère II," respectively. Although early experiences may be important for later development, they are not the sole determinants of outcome, as some investigators would have us believe. Bradley's longitudinal research indicates that later mothering behavior may have a greater impact on a child's intellectual functioning than mothering behavior during early infancy. The overemphasis on early mother-child interaction causes unnecessary guilt and fear in parents who believe they must be perfect in their early contacts with their child; this goal, of course, is unrealistic and can result in a sense of failure and perhaps less than optimal parenting thereafter. Successful parenting can have a positive impact at any point in development. In Sameroff's transactional perspective, parenting behavior interacts continually with the child's constitutional capacities throughout the course of development and is affected by social and cultural factors.

Robert A. Hoekelman, M.D.

BASIC ADAPTATIONS REQUIRED FOR SUCCESSFUL PARENTING

Stella Chess, M. D.

Chess believes that a complex interactional model is needed that takes into account the relationship between the child and his caretaking environment. She proposes that optimal development occurs when there is a "goodness of fit" between the child and the environment and that successful parenting depends upon parental sensitivity to this goodness of fit and the attempts of the parents to establish it. Understanding and knowing how to deal with differences in temperament in children can help parents establish goodness of fit with their child and reduce stress between the child and the system.

Chess begins by challenging two unidimensional ideas about parenting: (1) that there is one ideal way to be a parent, and (2) that the mother (or parent) is the cause of all current and eventual psychological disturbances in the child. She traces the evolution of these two related misconceptions, beginning with Freud's psycholanalytic theories in the 1920s, continuing with Watson's behaviorism through the psychiatric approach in the 1950s and 1960s, and through the attachment and bonding perspectives, which took hold in the 1970s and continue to influence thinking in the field. Adherents of each of these viewpoints consider their approach to explaining child development to be correct and believe that early childhood experiences, which almost universally involve the primary caregiver (usually the mother), have an irrevocable impact on future functioning. The enormous pressure on mothers created by this "blame-the-mother" ideology can result in stress that adversely affects parenting behavior.

Questioning the Blame-the-Mother Ideology

Chess and her associate, Dr. Alexander Thomas, began their major longitudinal studies of temperament in 1956 to revise the blame-the-mother or blame-the-parent ideology. The results of all longitudinal research on child development, including that carried out by Thomas and Chess, fail to support linear or blame-the-mother theories.

> With impressive unanimity, these studies have found that specific early life influences, including the mother's attitudes and child-care practices, are unreliable predictors of the child's later behavior and psychological characteristics.

Thus, to have attributed psychiatric disorders, both behavioral and emotional, mild and severe, primarily to the mother's early child-rearing attitudes and practices was a gross oversimplification and an incorrect assumption.

Although the mother's role in child development is significant, development proceeds through a series of interactions with many others, including the father, siblings, teachers, and peers. Other factors that influence child development include individual neurochemical, genetic, and temperamental characteristics. The point, then, that no one factor is overriding makes linear unidimensional models of child development obsolete.

A major negative feature of the blame-the-mother ideology (which evolved into the blame-the-parents ideology as the role of the father in child development fell under scrutiny) is the unnecessary and destructive guilt and anxiety suffered by mothers and fathers who believe that they must be perfect—a goal that is not within anyone's reach.

Although multidimensional views of development have been widely accepted, we have witnessed new formulations in the field during the past few years that reassert the crucial importance of the early mother-child relationship. Whereas earlier statements had placed the presumed critical period throughout the first five years of life, current formulations on attachment and bonding have moved this critical period to the first year and even to the first hours after birth. Chess cites leading advocates of the infant bonding thesis, who claim that the infant who fails to achieve a strong bond to the mother because she was not actively involved with him or her in the hours after birth or the infant who does not develop a secure attachment in subsequent months because the mother is insensitive to her infant's signals will develop behavioral or emotional problems. These involve a negative self-image, disturbance in task completion, and difficulties in future relationships. Chess goes on to cite and to support literature that challenges this thesis. Regarding the bonding, she concludes:

> The emphasis on the value of a strong early mother-neonate interaction has had a positive effect in opening hospital newborn nurseries to parents, but this campaign in no way requires or justifies categorical assertions about infant bonding that are not validated by the weight of research evidence and can only serve again to inflict unnecessary and destructive guilt and anxiety in a new generation of mothers.

Successful Parenting

The blame-the-parent ideology represents a major obstacle to successful parenting by instilling fear rather than providing realistic guidelines for healthy adaptation to new parental roles. Chess explains that this does not mean there are no bad parents. Some parents have serious psychological problems, irrational goals, or rigid, inflexible moral standards that can have serious consequences for their children's behavioral functioning and emotional development. Poor coping mechanisms and excessive stress can result in poor judgment and poor parenting. However, viewing the antecedents of normal function or of dysfunction within a linear or unitary model has not been shown to be valid and furthermore is potentially harmful.

> Physical medicine has long since freed itself from simplistic linear developmental models. A physically healthy start in life is better than a sickly childhood. But, we would never expect that the healthy six year old is invulnerable to future illness or that the undernourished, frail youngster is doomed to a life of chronic sickness. With psychological development, the genetic, maturational, and environmental contingencies and their interplay are even more complex and subject to greater variation and change than is physical development.

Chess expands on these ideas in the subsequent account of her research studies (conducted with Dr. Alexander Thomas) on temperament and its functional significance for child development. She describes how these studies led them to formulate the "goodness-of-fit" concept, a valuable model for identifying the critical elements in the parent-child interaction for any child at any given time.

Temperament and Its Functional Significance for Development

Chess and Thomas began their New York Longitudinal Study (NYLS) in 1956, when most developmental research dealt with either motivational, psychodynamic issues (the *why* of behavior) or with the psychometric testing of abilities (the *what* of behavior). Although these approaches advanced our knowledge of both normal and deviant psychological processes, Chess and Thomas believed that the *why* and *what* questions were insufficient lines of inquiry. Research and clinical evidence indicated that the *how* or the child's *style* of behavior also influenced responses to parental handling as well as parental attitudes. To answer these *how* questions, Chess and Thomas studied temperament.

They hypothesized that children's behavioral styles or individual temperaments could be distinguished from each other in systematic ways. Although differences in temperament in infants have been recognized by mothers, physicians, and nurses, study of these differences was neglected until the NYLS was instituted. Chess and Thomas identified three specific categories of temperament from the first months of life onward, defined criteria for assigning children to each category, and devised methods for quantifying ratings within each category.

Temperament was categorized in terms of nine characteristics: (1) activity level; (2) rhythmicity of biologic functions; (3) approach or withdrawal to new situations and stimuli; (4) ease of adaptability to change; (5) sensory threshold; (6) mood quality; (7) intensity of mood expressiveness; (8) distractibility; and (9) persistence and attention span.

Each of these nine characteristics was rated on a three-point scale: high, intermediate or variable, and low. By summing the quantified rating for each of the nine characteristics, three functionally significant clusters of child temperament were identified: the easy child, the difficult child, and the slow-to-warm-up child.

The *easy child* is described as one who is biologically regular, predominantly approaches rather than withdraws from new stimuli, adapts quickly, shows a generally positive mood, and has mild or moderate intensity of expression (40 percent of the sample).

The *difficult child* is at the opposite end of the spectrum and is described as one who is biologically irregular, has many withdrawal responses to new stimuli, adapts slowly, shows many negative mood responses, and has highly intense expressiveness of both negative and positive moods (10 percent of the sample).

The *slow-to-warm-up child* is described as similar to the difficult child with regard to withdrawal responses, slowness of adaptability, and negative mood responses, but this child has mild or moderate intensity of expressiveness and may or may not be biologically irregular (15 percent of the sample).

Chess and Thomas point out that individual children vary widely in the degree and sharpness with which they exhibit temperamental characteristics. The extent of the influence of the temperament on development and its consistency over time varies among children. In some instances, a child's temperament is remarkably consistent; in others, it shows moderate to marked change from one age to another.

Chess elaborated on temperamental consistency later in the conference when she presented preliminary NYLS follow-up data indicating high correlations between temperamental characteristics at three years of age and during young adulthood. Correlations were highest for adaptation scores and psychiatric diagnosis.

Parenting the Easy Child. Some children are easy to manage, and successful parenting is more likely. As infants, these children quickly establish regular sleep and feeding schedules, rapidly adjust to most new foods and new places, enjoy bathing from the beginning, and toilet train easily. Throughout infancy and childhood, their transitions from negative avoidance responses to positive adaptations in new situations occur quickly and smoothly; for example, adjustment to baby-sitters, new playmates, school attendance, and visits to strange places.

Chess emphasizes that because temperamental characteristics are not the only, and not necessarily the most important, determinants of future functioning, we must bear in mind that easy children can also develop behavior disorders. For example, when parents who were enrolled in the NYLS imposed special behavioral rules and standards on their easy children, who adapted without stress or resistance, serious problems developed because the behaviors displayed by these children conflicted with the standards of their peers and those imposed by the schools they attended.

Parenting the Difficult Child. Successful parenting of temperamentally difficult children is not easy, because new experiences typically evoke stormy protests. These children require skillful and patient channeling of their intense negative responses to new situations into positive responses. To accomplish this, parents must repeatedly expose the child to the same stimulus without insisting on immediate acceptance. With persistence and tolerance, as the new situation becomes more familiar to the child, positive adaptation will gradually occur. Chess points out that when these children are overly stressed, by unrealistic parental demands for immediate adaptation to new situations, by parental anger, or by punishment, they are at high risk for developing behavior disorders.

Chess indicates that just as the easy child is not immune to behavior disorders, the difficult child is not fated to develop one. The child's course to successful development depends more on parental adaptation to the child's temperament than on his temperament per se.

Parenting the Slow-to-Warm-Up Child. Parenting the slow-to-warm-up child is somewhat less difficult than parenting the difficult child. Biological rhythms in matters of sleep, eating, and elimination are normal in these children, and their negative reactions to new situations are expressed mildly. However, sometimes their negative responses and slow adaptations are interpreted as being due to timidity or anxiety, thus creating a self-fulfilling prophecy for these characteristics. Again, parental adaptation to the child's style will help the child to learn to adapt positively without unnecessary stress or negative social consequences. It is pointed out once more that many other factors may interact with the child's temperament to affect the process of development.

Goodness-of-Fit Model

The goodness-of-fit concept of parenting asserts that no single global formula can be applied to either parent or child to explain the origins or patterns of maladaptive behavior or emotional distress in any child. Temperament or parental attitudes and practices alone do not determine the course of a child's development. What is more decisive is the interaction of several important variables—those within the child and those within the parent. Goodness of fit is achieved when the properties of the environment (expectations and demands created outside the child) are consonant with the child's skills and potentials. Consonance between the child and the environment optimizes development. Conversely, dissonance between environmental demands and the child's temperamental characteristics creates a poorness of fit that can lead to maladaptive functioning and deviant development. Examples of dissonance in parenting include: demanding that an overly active child sit quietly throughout a long automobile ride; expecting a child of average intelligence to get all A's in school; overprotecting a physically handicapped child or denying the limitations imposed by that child's condition.

Chess does not believe that stress and conflict should be absent from a child's life. Without new and challenging expectations and opportunities to change and make decisions, a child's capacity for mastery and coping may not develop optimally. On the other hand, stress that is excessive or dissonant with the child's temperament and capabilities will result in poorness of fit and create even more stress. The cyclical and spiraling developmental dysfunction that grows from poorness of fit reflects the importance of examining many interactional variables over time, rather than viewing development in a linear fashion. This point was elaborated upon in various contexts throughout the conference.

Chess ended her presentation on an optimistic note:

> As the field of development studies has matured, we now have a much more optimistic vision of human development. The emotionally traumatized child is not doomed, the parents' early mistakes are not irrevocable, and our preventive and therapeutic intervention can make a difference at all age levels. This is perhaps the most important message we can transmit to the troubled parents who come to us for guidance and counseling.

SUCCESSFUL PARENTING IN THE BLACK COMMUNITY

Carol Ann Leal, M.D.

Leal rejects linear explanations of parenting and development. She enumerates many ingredients of successful parenting in the black community, including the promotion of self-esteem in children and the provision of useful and creative channels of gratification. She emphasizes the need to consider the sociological, political, and economic contexts within which children are raised and the impact of cultural stereotypes on black children. One path to overcoming the potential effects of negative images and irrational cultural beliefs on children has been for parents in the black community to acknowledge their existence and systematically direct their parenting efforts to establishing self-esteem in their children in spite of these obstacles.

There exists little information in the scientific literature that specifically addresses successful parenting in the black community. Leal explains that her approach to this controversial topic is influenced by her own personal biases and professional experiences. She provides a sociological perspective of how the black community is viewed in this country and how these perceptions can affect parenting. Leal poses the following six questions:

1. What is successful parenting?
2. Are there important differences between a parent who is black and one who is not?
3. What do we perceive the black community to be?
4. Given our conceptualizations and definitions, does successful parenting in the black community exist?
5. If and when it does, how might it be recognized or observed?
6. Once recognized, can the factors underlying successful parenting in the black community be delineated and applied in order to promote the welfare of this country?

To begin to answer these six questions, Leal offers a multifaceted definition of successful parenting in the form of two propositions: (1) Successful parenting is that state of being in which a single adult (or a pair of adults) has undertaken, by conscious choice or biological demand, the care and keeping of a child in such a manner that the child, by objective standards, is functioning optimally in accordance with his or her stage and phase of psychogenetic, psychosocial, emotional, adaptive, and temperamental development and in keeping with the capacities of his or her biological integrity and cognitive potential. (2) The success of parenting may be observable in the optimal functioning of the child at his or her levels of positive sense of self/other and manifestations of channels or avenues of gratification that are nondestructive to self or others. During each state, phase, and line of development, such a child, despite the stresses of the experience of living, exhibits a cohesive and readily observable pattern of behaviors in his or her experiences of and by the world through work (from schooling and chores through ultimate career achievement and socioeconomic autonomy); play (in the service of ego-enhancement through creativity); and in capacities for cultural continuity and contiguity, the establishment of empathy and of intimacy with others, and for biological continuity and contiguity.

The first proposition considers successful parenting in the context of a healthy, well-functioning family unit. The parents create an optimal environment, which provides the child with maximal opportunities for growth, good adaptation, emotional well-being, and the fulfillment of cognitive potential. Leal believes that this proposition is applicable to any parent who aspires to success in child-rearing, without racial distinction.

The second proposition considers the cultural context, which contains within it special stresses for minority groups, including the members of the black community. The particular issues in the second proposition that warrant special consideration when used in reference to black parents and children involve building self-esteem and finding appropriate and satisfying channels of gratification and creative expression. Leal explains that overt as well as subtle obstacles to the growth of self-esteem and to the search for gratifying outlets for self-expression have existed in our culture throughout history. The messages of "the genetic inferiority and part-object superiority of black people" are experienced consciously by blacks at all levels of society and education and in all locations, as these messages are unmistakable in their historical, political, literary, and scientific experience.

Leal describes the most current negative image of blacks as the fantasized identity of the "super black man" or "super black mother." Leal says of the super black mother:

> Regardless of the label given her, she remains a glittering sex object, an economic parasite, or a bearer of genetic and psychological inferiority.

These pervasive negative images of black people and black parents create a negative cultural context for the raising of black children. This negativism must be overcome by black parents in order for them to promote self-esteem in their children and provide them with nondestructive channels of gratification during childhood and into adulthood.

One reaction to these negative messages has been for blacks to seek alliance with other blacks and develop a sense of the black community. This seems to be an important way to combat the prejudices that are so vividly portrayed through the mass media and that have a devastating impact on black children. Leal believes that the acknowledgement of societal stereotypes, or irrational cultural beliefs, is the first step toward overcoming them. Black American parents who acknowledge the destructive images and themes that perpetuate role model myths attributed to blacks are more likely to be successful parents than those who do not. It is only through the recognition and acknowledgement that these myths exist that black parents can begin to eradicate the myths' pervasive influence on their children. Thus, promoting self-esteem and providing healthy channels of gratification for children involve the systematic effort of counteracting the effects of these negative messages.

Leal believes that black parents can be successful by being actively involved in their children's lives through guidance, limit-setting, work, play, sharing of social and cultural experiences, and through affectionate verbal and nonverbal exchange. This type of active, consistent involvement can help combat socialized racism and promote self-esteem in black children.

Open-Ended Interviews with Parents in the Black Community

To investigate successful parenting in the black community further, Leal developed and conducted open-ended interviews with a small sample of black single and married parents who she had observed to be unusually adept in their mastery of the demanding task of parenting. The sample consisted of two unmarried female parents and four married couples, who ranged in age from the early thirties to the mid-forties. All were self-supporting and represented working-class and middle-class providers, including members of the legal and medical professions. Their residences ranged from urban rental apartments and attached brownstones in predominantly black neighborhoods to middle- and upper-class single-family homes in predominantly white suburban communities. None of the school children attended public schools; their parents sent them to either integrated or segregated parochial or nonsectarian private schools. These particular families were chosen as subjects for interview on the basis of the unusually optimal functioning of the children in the areas of positive self/other esteem and constructive channels of gratification. By examining such families, Leal attempted to define further the ingredients of successful parenting.

The boys and girls ranged in age from 14 months through 19.5 years. They were characterized as "adaptively expending energy in a goal-directed manner with good discipline and age/stage/phase appropriate mastery." They enjoyed playing and did so creatively, both alone and with other children and adults. They enjoyed the company of other people and demonstrated behavior associated with high levels of confidence, assertiveness, and ability to share. When frustrated or angry, their withdrawal and outbursts were short-lived, and reestablishment of a positive mood and positive contact occurred.

Children who were old enough to be interviewed (those above three years of age) discussed, both spontaneously and when asked, important people in their lives (family members, parents, friends, parental friends, or characters in books), and their comments indicated a strong positive attachment and high regard for them. Older children shared their aspirations as future adults and parents and revealed their familiarity with the past and current roles of black people in many areas of distinction. In sum, the children in this sample were products of successful parenting, fulfilling the definitions presented earlier in Leal's two propositions.

Leal describes the family life of members of her sample as consisting of many close relationships with other black people. Close ties were maintained with family members through frequent contact by visits, by telephone, or by mail, regardless of the distance. Close friends, predominantly black, tended to assume surrogate family status in the lives of the families in the sample. The children in the sample were almost always included in family-oriented gatherings of relatives and close family friends.

In addition, all these parents, regardless of the formality or informality of their religious affiliations, provided their children with a strong religious identity. They felt that religion played a major role in their value systems, that a spiritual system within and beyond themselves often served as a source of security and inspiration, and that religion provided their children with channels of constructive gratification and useful coping mechanisms.

All of these factors—having close ties with family and friends, including children in gatherings with important members of their worlds, providing reasonable limits, providing a religious foundation, instilling the ingredients of high self-esteem, and providing constructive channels of gratification—contributed to the successful functioning of the children in the sample. Leal describes successful parenting in the black community as an uphill battle against forces deeply rooted in our culture but a goal that can be achieved through exercising great skill and patience.

FACTORS IN PREDICTING SUCCESSFUL PARENTING

Arnold J. Sameroff, Ph.D.

Beyond a *linear* model and even beyond an *interactional* model, Sameroff proposes a *transactional* model that takes time and the occurrence of continuing, dynamic events into account. Rather than examining constitutional and environmental variables in a static way, Sameroff explores how they might interact with and affect each other over time, that is, transactionally. He points out that socioeconomic status has accounted for more variance in child development than any other single variable but that we must keep in mind that this is a complex variable determined by many underlying factors. In his research on parenting, Sameroff explored parental levels of conceptualization of child development and found such levels to underlie differential outcomes based on socioeconomic status. Like Leal, Sameroff also stresses the need for systematic exploration of social and political influences on parenting and development.

In keeping with the spirit and underlying philosophies of Chess and Leal, Sameroff also rejects unitary explanations of successful parenting. For many years, the potential impact of parental attitudes was the main focus of researchers in the area of development. However, much of this early work neglected to take into account that one underlying factor, such as a particular parental attitude, may be associated with many different outcomes, just as many different underlying factors might result in the same outcome. Sameroff believes that many variables included under biological and environmental factors interact over time to affect development and that these variables need to be studied from more than a psychological perspective. In addition to psychology and education, the disciplines of sociology, anthropology, and economics provide a broader context for examining the complex process of development.

The Continuum of Caretaking Causality: The Organism-Environment Relationship

In 1975, Sameroff and his colleague, Michael Chandler, were engaged in a research project on the role of perinatal factors, such as low birth weight, anoxia, and neurological signs, in developmental deviancy. At that time, neither the scientific literature nor the ongoing work of these investigators found clear links between perinatal factors and later behavioral or emotional disorders. The most significant variable in predicting developmental outcome turned out to be socioeconomic status, which accounted for approximately 25 percent of the variance from birth to four years of age. Whether or not perinatal factors were related to later deficits depended on the economic and social conditions of the family as a whole; that is, birth complications were linked to problems in later development when the children in question came from poor families. Thus, the constitution of the organism by itself was an insufficient predictor of developmental outcome. The caretaking environment, including educational, emotional, and economic conditions, must also be taken into account. Sameroff and Chandler (1975) proposed a *continuum of caretaking causality* to describe the interaction between the constitutionally at-risk organism and the environment.

> At one end of the continuum, the caretaking environment was sufficiently supportive and adaptive to compensate for almost any biological risk factor, so that it was not transformed into later intellectual or emotional problems. At the other end of the continuum, the caretaking environment had neither the educational, emotional, nor economic resources to deal with even the slightest perinatal problem. Thus, the child, if allowed to survive, would maintain deficits into later stages of intellectual and emotional growth.

Sameroff points out that any single-factor model is too simplistic and static to be useful. Furthermore, an interactive model, combining constitutional and environmental factors in an additive fashion, does not describe these factors in dynamic terms as they change over time. In order to account for the continual interplay of a changing organism and a changing environment, a transactional model is needed. A simple interactional model explains neither how a good constitution plus a good environment can lead to poor outcomes nor how a bad constitution plus a bad environment can lead to good outcomes. A transactional model does account for these types of combinations by examining changes over time rather than states and events fixed in time (Figure 1).

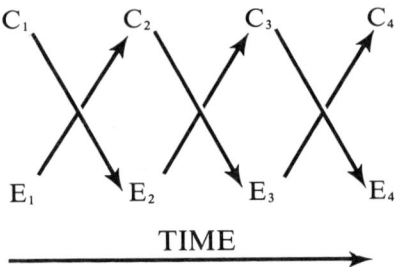

Figure 1. Transactional model.

A transactional model is also flexible enough to account for discontinuities in development, such as the disappearance of early deviances later in development. These discontinuities have been referred to as the self-righting tendencies of the organism.

Self-righting tendencies can come from the child or from the caretaking environment. Examples of self-righting tendencies from the child's side include blind and deaf children achieving normal cognitive and social skills in spite of their handicaps and thalidomide infants achieving their cognitive development through the coordination of remaining parts of their limbs. The positive development of handicapped children indicates very strong self-righting tendencies. The retardation found in such infants was correlated less with their degree of handicap than with their degree of social isolation. This was particularly noticeable with language skills, because very often no one talks to these children.

The self-righting tendencies in the caretaking environment, particularly in interaction with those of the child, can account for qualitative differences in the performance of children. Sameroff believes that environmental self-righting tendencies are just beginning to be explored. He presents his most current theoretical views and research directed toward defining relevant variables.

Parental Concepts of Development

Because socioeconomic status has been such a pervasive and significant factor in developmental research, Sameroff attempts to examine this variable to determine its components. One aspect of this work has focused on parental attitudes and values, the impact of culture on parental perceptions, different norms and expectations that influence individuals in different social classes, and social class differences in child-rearing behavior and life experiences. Because these factors may be related to developmental outcome, Sameroff believes that it is important to investigate these areas more thoroughly, particularly parental cognition, which may account for a large part of the impact of socioeconomic status. To do this, Sameroff designed an assessment tool (Concepts of Development Questionnaire) that attempts to pinpoint the underlying theories parents hold concerning child development.

Based on Piaget's concepts, Sameroff theorized that, as in the cognition of developing children, parents' cognition varies along a continuum from concrete to abstract, from egocentric to self/other considerations, and from one-track to multifaceted. Parenting at the lower end of the continuum may present problems for developmental outcome in children who are at risk or handicapped.

Four levels of parental perspectives were postulated and used as the basis for items in the Concepts of Development Questionnaire: (1) symbiotic, (2) categorical, (3) compensating, and (4) perspectivistic.

The Symbiotic Level. Parents at the symbiotic, or lower, end of the continuum are typically atheoretical in their understanding of child development. Like Piaget's sensory motor-level infant model, this type of parent (usually the mother) responds in a here-and-now manner, not truly differentiating herself from her baby. For example, if breast-feeding feels good for the mother, she assumes it is good for the baby. Because cognition at this level is intertwined with emotional involvement, it is not possible for the mother to differentiate herself from the child nor to reflect on the process of development.

Items on the Concepts of Development Questionnaire designed to elicit symbiotic level responses were based on immediate emotional reactions to the child. For example, "A mother is very happy when she gets her baby to smile;" "Mothers feel upset if they cannot get their babies to look at them;" "She cannot get along with kids or teachers."

The Categorical Level. Parents at the categorical, or second, level can differentiate themselves from the child and can, to some extent, consider the causes of determinants of developmental outcome. Like Piaget's preoperational child model, the categorical parent considers only one influence for any particular situation. The tendency at this level is to label children and thereby stereotype their course of development. For example, "Fussy babies will grow up to be disagreeable;" "He was born with intellect;" "Boy babies are more active than girl babies."

The Compensating Level. At the third, or compensating, level the parent is able to differentiate the child from the labels applied to the child. As in Piaget's concrete operational child model, the compensating parent is able to coordinate different dimensions and can thus consider two or more developmental influences for a specific outcome. This may involve constitutional influences and environmental influences, two constitutional influences, or two environmental influences. Although a full appreciation of the relationship between a variable and an outcome is lacking, a parent at this level can appreciate how one environmental event could affect two children differently.

Items on the Concepts of Development Questionnaire concerning compensation attempted to get at age/behavior coordinations and an awareness of the interaction of constitution and environment in influencing developmental outcomes. Examples of such items include: "The most difficult child may be helped by a combination of good parental care, the right kind of schooling, and proper medical attention;" "Some children take a lot longer than others to learn how to control their bowels."

The Perspectivistic Level. Parents at the fourth, or perspectivistic, level are able to place their children and particular circumstances of development within a hypothetical context. As in Piaget's formal operational adult, the perspectivistic parent is able to consider a vast array of possibilities and their potential relationships to any particular situation. These parents can give a comprehensive explanation of the complex process of development, viewing the child's development as taking place within the context of a dynamic system of relationships involving many variables. Rather than a child's problem being viewed as having one constitutional or environmental source (e.g., "He was born rotten or spoiled"), problems are explained by a combination of events over time (transactionally); for example, "If his grandmother had not died when he was four and I had not gotten divorced three years later, Johnny would not be so upset now. But if I can stabilize his emotional life and settle down, I am sure he will turn out all right." Generally, the responses of the perspectivistic parents lack the static character seen in responses of parents at lower levels. Thus, perspectivistic parents may be described as changing along with their children.

Research on Parental Concepts of Development

The large differences in child competencies found among groups differing in social status raise the question of whether parents of different socioeconomic status differ in their concepts of development. If concepts of development vary with socioeconomic status, then one important factor underlying socioeconomic differences will have been uncovered. The results of Sameroff's study of four-year-old children and their mothers* were encouraging, because the data began to explain why children raised by parents from different social classes were turning out differently—it had to do with the ways in which parents thought about their children.

Each national sample was divided into an upper and a lower social status group. As hypothesized, mothers in lower socioeconomic groups agreed more with the categorical items and less with the compensating and perspectivistic items than did mothers from higher socioeconomic groups. Interestingly, social class interacted with cultural heritage, so that the English upper class group with the capacity for perspectivistic thinking chose to "stay in its place" and overrode these higher abilities by agreeing with categorical items.

Once socioeconomic status and cultural differences were established, Sameroff investigated the impact of different cognitive orientations on developmental outcomes. About 200 of the American families in the sample participated in a four-year longitudinal study of their children. At the four-year follow-up, the children were assessed to determine their developmental status. The performance of the children was correlated with maternal scores on the Concepts of Development Questionnaire. Significant correlations revealed relationships between a mother's concepts of development and a child's performance in the intellectual, social, and emotional do-

---

* There was a total of 483 mothers, of whom 145 were from England and 338 from the United States.

mains. Mothers with underdeveloped cognitive abilities had children at age four with lower IQs, lower perceptual abilities, and poorer social and emotional adaptation than children of mothers with high levels of cognition.

To confirm these findings, Sameroff attempted an open-ended examination of parental perspectives by creating several vignettes about children's behavior that reflected developmental problems and then testing a group of mothers varying in social class and child-rearing experience. The mothers were asked to explain the behavior of the children in the stories. Their explanations were scored according to a predetermined coding system, which discriminated among the four levels of concepts of development. As found in previous work, social class and level of education were clearly reflected in the explanations given by the mothers.

Sameroff raises the broader issue of identifying which forces move individuals to higher levels of developmental perspective and which forces limit advances in others. One limitation can be attributed to individual cognitive abilities, since those individuals who do not generally use abstract, hypothetical thinking would not be expected to use it for developmental issues. Another possible limitation may be that developmental trends are often culturally defined. For example, if the society functions categorically, as Spartans did by letting female babies die or as nomadic tribes did by killing twins because they were considered evil, then it is difficult for individual members of that culture to function at high levels. Sameroff suggests the need for more thorough study of the sociology of development.

Parental Reactions to Developmental Progressions

Developmental progressions can come as a welcome or unwelcome surprise to parents. Findings at the symbiotic level, based on frequent clinical observations of mothers, reveal that many emotionally immature mothers thrive with a dependent and responsive infant. However, when the child enters the exploratory phase—walking and seeking autonomy—these mothers tend to resist their child's new independence, even though it is a sign of healthy development. At this point, a period of abuse may ensue, frequently ending with the child being placed in a foster home and the same mother soon pregnant again.

Emotionally mature mothers with high levels of cognitive functioning welcome the development of autonomous functioning in their children. Clinical observations of such mothers reveal a pattern in which early mother-infant interactions may be cool, with more intense, synchronous interactions as the child becomes more autonomous.

Thus, the ways in which parents interpret and react to their children's developmental changes depend to some extent on parental levels in conceptualizing the developmental process. The greater the extent to which the parent perceives the child as a separate human being with a variety of internal and external stimuli impinging upon him or her, the greater the extent to which the parent will look forward to and appreciate the child's reaching important developmental milestones.

> The way in which parents think about their children should have an important impact on the way they will behave toward their children and ultimately on the developmental outcomes for those children. For example, parents who see individual differences as rooted in the nature of the child should make less use of remedial or therapeutic programs than should parents who see their children's behavior as being strongly influenced by environmental contingencies. The documentation of these differences in parental perspectives on developmental outcomes would add a redundant dimension to the prediction and understanding of children's development.

SUMMARY COMMENTS

Robert Bradley, Ph.D.

Bradley summarized the major points made in the presentations by Chess, Leal, and Sameroff on successful parenting and discussed their implications for high-risk parenting. He also presented data from his longitudinal study on the impact of early experience on behavioral and intellectual development and suggested areas for further investigation, including the analysis of developmental transactions.

Bradley believes that the presentations on successful parenting represent "a eulogy for the simple linear relationship" and "a eulogy for the exclusive predominance of maternal effect—perhaps most directly stated by Stella Chess." With regard to linear explanations of child development, Bradley feels that the evidence for abandoning the simple cause-effect model of development was convincingly and unanimously made by the presenters: Sameroff concerning children at early biologic risk, Chess concerning the risk of psychiatric disorders among children with different temperaments, and Leal concerning successful parenting in black families. Sameroff offers, instead, the transactional model, which views developmental outcome as resulting from the dynamic interactions of constitutional and environmental variables over time. Chess offers an interactional view, with temperamental variables playing a major role in affecting parenting and with parents establishing "goodness of fit" between the caretaking environment and the functioning of the child. Leal also offers an interactional model in which cultural, historical, and political variables play a major role in parenting and development. Thus, there are no simple linear relationships between the type of parenting given a child and the developmental outcomes for the child.

The second myth—that early experiences, particularly with the mother, have a lasting and pronounced effect on development—is also challenged by the presenters, including Bradley. The unique input of early experience is being re-evaluated by a number of investigators, including Michael Rutter (also cited by Chess), who concluded that, contrary to the belief that mother-infant contact immediately after birth was critical to mother's development of a strong bond with the baby, "...it is clear that both mothers and fathers can, and commonly do, develop strong attachments to their children in the absence of neonatal contact."

Bradley underscores the importance of exploring parenting and child development within the context of broader disciplines, which was emphasized by Sameroff and Leal. Sameroff considers as crucial a socioeconomic perspective and the factors underlying this multifaceted variable. Leal believes that it is not possible to talk about or to examine parenting in the black community without addressing the impact of cultural stereotyping.

Longitudinal Study of the Impact of Early Experience on Development

Bradley's research on the impact of maternal behavior on intellectual development corroborates the point that early experience, by itself, is not always the critical determining factor in the development of most children. He and his colleagues have been engaged in a longitudinal study for the past ten years investigating the relationship between family environment and child development.

The subjects included 135 families who were periodically assessed in their homes by means of the HOME Inventory, which was developed for this research. Other data collected on the sample include scores on mental tests (Bayley scores in the first two years of life and Stanford-Binet scores thereafter). The HOME Inventory is a 45-item scale with items clustered into six subscales. The six subscales, with one sample item from each, are as follows:

1. **Emotional and verbal responsiveness of mother.** Sample item: Mother caresses or kisses child at least once during visit.
2. **Acceptance of child.** Sample item: Mother does not interfere with child's actions or restrict child's movements more than three times during visit.
3. **Organization of physical and temporal environment.** Sample item: Child's play environment appears safe and free of hazards.
4. **Provision of appropriate play materials.** Sample item: Mother provides toys or interesting activities for child during interview.
5. **Maternal involvement with child.** Sample item: Mother tends to keep child within visual range and to look at the child often.

6. **Opportunities for variety in daily stimulation.** Sample item: Child eats at least one meal per day with mother and father.

Information needed to score the scale was obtained through a combination of observation and interview of the child's primary caregiver, done in the home when the child was present and awake. The investigators found that infant scores on the HOME Inventory were highly correlated with children's mental test scores later in life. As Table 1 shows, the correlations between HOME scores and three-year-old children's Stanford-Binet scores were moderate to high.

As seen in Table 1, the correlations between HOME scores and IQ increased as the time of HOME assessment approached the time of IQ assessment. The same pattern held with regard to HOME scores and IQ scores of 54-month-old children. In addition, correlations shown in Table 1 are rather high, with the correlation between the 24-month HOME scores and the IQs of 36-month-old children at 0.70 accounting for 49 percent of the variance.

Table 1. Correlations between HOME Scores and IQs of 36-Month-Old Children

HOME Scores	Time of HOME Assessment		
	6 months	12 months	24 months
Responsiveness	0.25	0.39	0.50
Acceptance	0.24	0.24	0.41
Organization	0.40	0.39	0.41
Toys	0.41	0.56	0.64
Involvement	0.33	0.47	0.55
Variety	0.31	0.28	0.50
Total score	0.50	0.55	0.70
Multiple correlation	0.54	0.59	0.72

At this point in the study, the investigators questioned whether the high correlation between early environmental scores and later developmental scores reflected the importance of early environment or whether the correlations resulted as an artifact of high correlations between early and later HOME scores. Partial correlational analyses were therefore performed. Bradley calculated the partial correlation between six-month HOME scores and IQs of three-year-old children controlling for twelve-month HOME scores. The results, presented in Table 2, indicated that when twelve-month HOME scores were parceled out, there was little residual correlation between six-month HOME scores and IQs of 36-month-old children. By contrast, the partial correlation between twelve-month HOME score and IQs of 36-month-old children was significant when controlling for six-month HOME score. A less-pronounced effect was observed when 12- and 24-month HOME scores were compared.

Table 2. Partial Correlations between HOME Scores and IQs of 36-Month-Old Children

HOME Subscales	Six-Month HOME and IQ Controlling for Twelve-Month HOME		Twelve-Month HOME and IQ Controlling for Six-Month HOME	
	Male	Female	Male	Female
Responsiveness	0.07	0.01	0.27	0.49
Acceptance	0.20	0.03	0.03	0.37
Organization	0.25	0.12	0.40	0.46
Toys	0.39	0.19	0.61	0.55
Involvement	0.05	0.09	0.41	0.53
Variety	0.24	0.23	0.19	0.42
Total score	0.21	0.04	0.36	0.53

These results have important implications for the field of high-risk parenting. The data support the thesis that child development cannot be explained by simple causal relationships and that early experiences are not always critical and lasting. As Chess has proposed, the guilt and anxiety felt by many mothers who believe they must be perfect can be relieved. In terms of implications for intervention, these data support the view that in trying to meet the child's needs we need not focus all our efforts on fostering the early mother-infant bond, but rather, we can adjust time frames and approaches for each individual set of needs. When dealing with the mother-child relationship, a long-term view might be taken—that is, assisting mothers who are unprepared or prevented from mothering in becoming effective as their relationships with their children develop. In addition to, or as an alternative to, working on the mother-child relationship, broader approaches eliciting support from a larger social network, including fathers and the extended family, might prove useful.

Bradley notes that many of the research studies available do not deal with extreme environments, which are key in contributing to high-risk parenting. Therefore, inferences about high-risk parenting cannot be made, and their data often cannot be generalized.

Exploring the Transactional Model

> In his discussion of the relation between early risk factors and poor developmental outcomes, Sameroff has unceremoniously laid to rest the value of single-factor and interactional models. He suggests that a transactional model (one that views development as a dynamic interplay between the changing organism and the changing environment) more accurately explains developmental deviancy. This model is gradually effecting changes both in our research on human development and in the strategies used to promote development in high-risk situations.

Although the field is beginning to adopt the transactional perspective, Bradley is concerned that this approach may be mistaken for an interactional position. According to Bradley, interactional models are improvements over linear, simple cause-effect explanations of phenomena in that they take into account a combination of factors when predicting outcome. However, interactional models view these combinations in an additive fashion; for example, considering the effects of perinatal complications *in addition to* an impoverished environment, rather than viewing the complex interplay of these variables over time. Interactional models do not conceptualize developmental problems as stemming from *synergistic* combinations of factors over time. Without a synergistic perspective, interactional models are actually linear, even though not unitary.

Unfortunately, few research studies use a truly synergistic approach to design or analyze data. This is partly because of the limitations imposed by statistical behavioral analyses, which are primarily designed to answer linear and interactional questions. This situation is improving, however, with behavioral scientists making more creative use of existing multivariate techniques and with new methods being developed. Bradley believes that he and his colleagues are also guilty of not thoroughly investigating developmental roots and outcomes using a transactional perspective. However, he presents a series of cross-lagged panel analyses and bivariate correlations that reveal something of a dynamic interplay between home environmental factors and children's mental test performance at ages 6, 12, and 24 months.

One of the most important components of Sameroff's transactional model is that of self-righting tendencies, both in the organism and in the environment. By including the dynamic interplay of organism and environment, complexity of causation, and self-righting tendencies, the transactional model is similar to a general systems model.

> The child is seen as a product of a system of units that interact. The system is composed of a number of units, each interacting in complex ways with the other units. Within this framework, the child is seen as an active organism, eliciting responses from the environment at the same time he or she is adapting to its demands. Within the child, cybernetic processes operate to regulate behavior. In essence, the child is continuously trying to adapt to the environment. Each variable within the particular system has a range of stability. That stability is maintained in equilibrium by transactions with the environment and the system. Any variable that forces the system beyond its range of stability is called a stress, producing strain in the system.

The organism as a complex system trying to adapt to the demands of a larger external system has been conceptualized in different ways by the three presenters on successful parenting—in Leal's comments on the historical, political context that impinges on black families; in Sameroff's transactional model; and in the "goodness-of-fit" concept articulated by Chess.

Bradley emphasizes the need for further research on the transactional or general systems model, so that we can eventually understand the relationships between parental conceptions of the developmental process and actual developmental outcomes and between significant antecedents and outcomes. Bradley agrees with Sameroff that we must begin to identify those forces that limit advance in this area in order to overcome them. Two such limitations include inadequate statistical techniques and narrow perspectives. Accurate, in-depth environmental measurement is critical for advancement of the transactional model, and it would be most useful if the designs and data collection were based on a perspectivistic view of parenting and development.

PART II
HIGH-RISK PARENTING

The papers comprising Part II address the complex issues of high-risk parenting. The types of questions posed and investigated include: How do pregnancy and the birth of a child affect women, men, and couples? What characteristics in the child or in the parent increase the likelihood of dysfunctional parenting and poor developmental outcomes? How does the birth of an infant who is premature or medically impaired affect parenting? How do parents handle the death of a child, and how does their tragedy affect their marriage and their future parenting? What are the risks of adolescent parenting? How does psychological impairment of the parents influence their behavior? How do parents who abuse or neglect their children differ from those who do not? What are the interrelations among the pediatric social illnesses? How do parental conceptions about their role and about children affect parenting? How can health professionals prevent high-risk parenting or intervene when it exists?

The ten presenters in Part II represent a wide variety of professions, including educators, sociologists, an economist, social workers, pediatricians, an obstetrician/gynecologist, psychologists, psychiatrists, and nurses. They all presented clinical research data relevant to the questions stated above. Although coming from different disciplines and orientations, there was a high level of consensus in terms of underlying philosophies of child development and parenting, the feasibility of interactional approaches, and the need for more in-depth research and more effective strategies for prevention and intervention.

Robert A. Hoekelman, M.D.

COPING WITH PREGNANCY AND PARENTHOOD

Howard J. Osofsky, M.D., Ph.D.[1]

Introduction

Osofsky conceptualizes expectant and new parenthood as a major developmental phase for the mother and father, both as individuals and as a couple. In his presentation, he examines the factors involved in their adaptation to pregnancy and the potential impact of this crisis on the marital relationship and on the new child. He also presents the concerns of expectant parents whose circumstances require special adjustment to the processes of pregnancy and new parenthood. These special groups include older parents, stepparents, isolated parents with few supports, and parents of atypical children.

Osofsky views the processes of pregnancy and new parenthood as stressful transitional periods that require serious adjustments, not only for the expectant mother but also for the expectant father and the couple as a unit. Like other developmental and maturational processes, pregnancy is a period of transition, which can result in either positive growth or regression. Successful outcome or resolution of this period depends on numerous factors, which influence adjustment to both the idea and the reality of an infant. Up to this point, the literature has focused primarily on the expectant mother. The expectant father and couple have been neglected areas of inquiry.

Examination of the impact of pregnancy and new parenthood on fathers and couples is critical because of the potential contributions of this developmental period to marital and family dysfunction. The arrival of a new infant does not merely enlarge the family but initiates a major set of effects on the functioning of each individual and the whole family as a system.

---

[1] The studies described herein were conducted by Dr. Osofsky in collaboration with Joy D. Osofsky, Ph.D.

Adjustments for the Woman

Like puberty and menopause, pregnancy is a period of transition for a woman because of the profound psychological and physical changes that occur so rapidly. This is true of both first and subsequent pregnancies. As in all human crises, the outcome is dependent not only on the long-standing personality patterns of the woman but also on her current life situation, including the existence or absence of helping figures in the family and environment and the availability of services in the community. It has been shown that intervention, both in the planning and process phases of pregnancy, can be extremely effective in promoting and safeguarding the relationship of the mother to her future child as well as other relationships among family members.

Osofsky's clinical work and research endeavors have shed light on some of the major concerns of expectant mothers: fears and anxieties about pregnancy, labor, and delivery; concerns about body functioning and body image; coping with considerable emotional liability; rethinking of their relationships with their own mothers; conflicts about dependency and the joys and demands of motherhood; and reassessments of their relationships with their husbands. Developmental issues and current life situations play roles in determining the nature of these struggles and their outcomes. Osofsky points out that ignoring these changes and subsequent adjustments can lead to further conflicts and adjustment difficulties for both the woman and her family. A more immediate concern is the potential impact of the expectant woman's psychological adjustment on the process of pregnancy itself.

Research has revealed significant relationships between patterns of difficulty in coping and the course of labor and delivery. Negative psychological adjustment may contribute to pregnancy difficulties. In addition, mothers who, late in pregnancy, are characterized as anxious or showing poor adaptation to pregnancy typically receive more pain-relieving medication during labor and delivery. High levels of tension have been associated with various complications during labor and delivery.

What factors underlie extreme emotional reactions to pregnancy and childbearing? Studies have revealed two key factors. The first is described as maternal role conflict between success outside the home in a profession and success in the home as a mother. The second factor involves personal insecurity related less to playing the maternal role than to dwelling on past losses, hurt, and failures. Emotional stress can also be heightened by lack of assistance, guidance, and support in the current environment.

What can be done to alleviate high levels of stress? Instruction directed toward reorganizing attitudes and activities related to motherhood has produced long-term favorable effects, sometimes with benefits lasting throughout a four-to six-year period following the mother's pregnancy. In addition, women who are better prepared for the motherhood role generally enjoy healthier and better adjusted lives with fewer marital and social conflicts. Information provided by the woman's own doctor and by nurses is typically more effective than classroom instruction.

An important theme in women's adjustment to pregnancy is the continual interplay between mental and bodily processes. Anxiety, moodiness, depression, and overdependency are associated with physical complaints and problems. Although it is difficult to establish the existence of direct causal relationships, the impact of the mind on the body and vice versa warrants further study for a more complete understanding of women's adjustment to the pregnancy process.

Adjustments for the Man

Osofsky points out that in comparison to the focus on expectant motherhood, considerably less attention has been paid to the psychological aspects of expectant fatherhood. The work that has been done in this neglected area has concentrated on the emotional difficulties that men experience during their wives' pregnancies rather than on the developmental processes that men go through at this stressful time in their lives. Consequently, there has been a tendency to minimize the special adjustments that normal men make in response to pregnancy and new parenthood.

As is the case for women, this period of transition can result in either maturation or regression, depending on such factors as the quality of earlier family relationships, degree of open communication with their wives, and knowledge about the pregnancy and parenting processes. Unresolved past relationships with parents and siblings can precipitate the emergence of new conflicts in the current stressful situation. Often, the men who develop emotional difficulties at this time had unfulfilled dependency needs as a child and now place more demands on their wives for attention and nurturance. This dynamic often has a negative impact on both the husband-wife relationship and the psychological environment of the infant. Lack of knowledge or misinformation about pregnancy and parenthood can add to the stress on men and their relationships with the family. It is important to deal with these conflicts and deficits to help men in their transition to fatherhood.

Adjustments for the Couple

Significant changes in the marital relationship often begin during pregnancy and continue throughout the parent-child relationship. These changes are related to, but separate from, the changes that take place within each individual of the marital dyad. Osofsky believes that it is crucial to examine more carefully the adjustments that occur within the individuals and in the marital relationship during pregnancy and following childbirth. By doing so, it may be possible to learn how this period in life can be used as a maturational phase leading to optimal growth for the couple and the family rather than as a destructive and disintegrating experience.

In examining these issues, it is relevant to take into account the changing social phenomena, which can have an impact on the functioning of the family. These include: shifts in patterns of adolescent sexuality and pregnancy; alteration in concepts about family planning and family size; advances in contraceptive techniques and more readily available abortions; alterations in family structure and family and community supports; increases in the divorce rate, with an accompanying rise in the number of single-parent families; and growing numbers of women entering the work force. These social changes and pressures should be taken into account in the study of the pregnancy phase.

Couples most apt to get through this period successfully possess or learn various strategies. They are able to negotiate and solve problems together, which enables them to seek alternative means for mutual gratification. They are able to reserve time for each other without letting the infant pervade all aspects of their marital life. These skills and strategies can be taught to all expectant parents, but especially to those at risk. Level of functioning at this time depends on the availability of such training as well as on the preexisting degree of marital discord, parental expectations, and temperament of the infant. The prevention of potential stress for the couple is a neglected area of inquiry.

Adjustments for the Older Parent

Increasing numbers of couples are choosing to become parents at a later age. It is no longer uncommon for a woman to become pregnant for the first time in her late thirties or even early to mid-forties. Osofsky describes a number of factors related to this trend. Some women who had decided against having children changed their minds as they became aware of menopause in the not-too-distant future. Some individuals remarried at a later age following the divorce of one or both partners. Some individuals wanted to establish a professional career or gain financial security before becoming parents. This latter factor seems to be a major one in the decision to have a child at a later age. Many couples feel less concerned about the freedom they will be giving up since they have accomplished many of their financial and professional goals.

Most of the older couples that Osofsky has seen have been pleased about their expectant or new parenthood, conveying feelings of warmth and security in their new roles. However, there are special concerns with which older couples must deal to resolve the pregnancy and parenthood experiences in a positive way. Medically, older women must confront the issues of high incidences of prenatal, labor, and delivery complications and the risk of Down syndrome. Older couples may also have concerns about their own health, both currently and as their child is growing up.

In addition to medical concerns, there are psychological adjustments that must be made. The expectant mother and father may experience mixed feelings about the pregnancy. They may worry about what their friends will think. Their friends may have diverging interests, since their own children may be almost grown. Expectant parents may be aware of and concerned about their energy levels decreasing as they grow older. They may be especially aware of the increased noise levels in their environment after the birth of children. They may have fewer support systems (e.g., parents of their own) than younger couples. Thus, the special joys of older parenthood are mixed with special concerns.

Adjustments for the Stepparent

When the current marriage has followed a divorce or when there are children from the previous marriage, the couple is exposed to special pressures. Some of these pressures are socially based, but more often they are internal. They want things to be better this time; that is, they want the marriage to be more secure, and they want the children from the previous marriage to do well.

During the pregnancy phase, the couple may either feel a greater sense of union and security or experience the fear that this marriage may also end in divorce. In Osofsky's clinical experience, a number of pregnant wives have expressed worries that their husbands will leave them with a child and little financial support, especially if their husbands are already paying alimony or child support or are in conflict with ex-wives over such payments.

At the time of remarriage, most couples plan to treat children from a previous marriage as their joint children. However, in many cases problems arise that undermine this plan. Some of the obstacles include the bond between these children and their biological parents, pressures from former spouses, and the birth of a jointly conceived child.

One woman recently told us of her experience in which her husband had looked forward to being, and then initially felt like, a father to her two children from a previous marriage. However, when she became pregnant with their jointly conceived child, he began to refer to the children as her children and the new infant as their child, a practice he never dropped. Years later when grandchildren were born, he referred to them as her grandchildren. In our experience this reaction has been a common one, at least on an emotional level.

Sometimes couples in this group try to solve their problems by moving to a new community, viewing this as the beginning of a new life without pressures from the former spouse or, at times, from the children of the previous marriage.

Adjustments for the Isolated Parent

There is an increasing number of isolated parents with little outside support. As couples leave their home communities for educational and career opportunities, they become isolated from family and friends. Their support systems are reduced, and this can create a level of stress that puts some couples at risk. In isolated geographical areas there may also be an absence of community resources, which adds to the burden during the crises of pregnancy and new parenthood.

Osofsky believes that the pressures of isolation and lack of traditional support can lead to serious difficulties both within the marriage and for the family as a whole. He urges the development of strategies for assistance to isolated couples at risk.

Adjustments for the Unprepared Parent

Expectant couples have certain preconceptions concerning the processes of pregnancy and birth and the state of their newborn child. When these expectations are violated because of unforeseen events, special stresses are created.

For example, increasing numbers of couples have been choosing to deliver in birthing centers or at home. If a completely spontaneous natural delivery is not possible, a considerable number of women then feel like failures, experiencing inappropriate feelings of guilt.

Another event for which parents are usually unprepared is the birth of a premature infant. Misconceptions and guilt about this can influence the infants condition adversely, which in turn can affect parental reactions to the infant. Osofsky has found that parents can be better prepared with prenatal intervention, which can help broaden the range of parental expectations and teach parents how to provide specialized care if needed.

THE VULNERABLE DYAD— ADOLESCENT MOTHERS AND THEIR INFANTS

Elizabeth R. McAnarney, M.D.[1]

Introduction

McAnarney summarizes key data on risk factors associated with adolescent childbearing. Variables affecting obstetric and neonatal

---

[1] The studies described herein were conducted by Dr. McAnarney in collaboration with Marilyn J. Aten, R.N., M.S. and Ruth A. Lawrence, M.D. These studies were supported by a Gerber Medical Grant-in-Aid and National Institute of Mental Health Contract # 81 M053662401D.

outcome and psychological functioning are discussed. In addition, McAnarney presents her current research on the nature of adolescent mother-infant interaction. The data from this investigation suggest that the adolescent mother at highest risk of parental dysfunction is a 15-16-year-old, non-black, lower-socioeconomic-status adolescent. McAnarney concludes with a series of questions to which she believes future research in this area should be addressed.

The numbers of births and the birth rates to adolescent females have been of major concern to health-care providers. The proportion of children born to teenagers from 1960 to 1970 increased from 14 percent to 17 percent. During the same period of time, the birth rate to women (births per thousand women) fell from 91.0 to 69.7 percent. This increase in births to females aged 15 to 19 disappeared during the 1970s, except for one age group, the mother less than 15 years of age.

In 1978, the birth rates were higher for non-white than for white adolescents. The ratio of non-white to white was highest at age 14 and lowest at age 19. Although the illegitimacy rate for black women aged 15 to 19 has not changed substantially, it has increased 26.6 percent for white women. As a rough estimation, one-third of all abortions in the United States have been performed for adolescents, numbering approximately 400,000 in 1978.

Obstetrical Outcome for Adolescent Mothers and Their Infants

The age of the mother is only one of many variables that affect the birth of the infant. McAnarney presents a host of other factors that could potentially affect obstetrical outcome (Table 1).

McAnarney concludes from the available data that if adolescents receive early and consistent prenatal care, they should not have poorer obstetrical outcomes than adults of similar parity, race, or socioeconomic and marital status. However, there is still some question whether adolescents are more likely to experience hypertensive disease during pregnancy. Furthermore, infants born to adolescents should not experience greater morbidity than infants matched for similar status.

There has been some question as to whether women less than 15 years of age are more likely to bear babies weighing less than 2500 g than adult women of similar backgrounds. In 1971 and 1977, two reports suggested the closer the very young mother was to her menarche at the time of delivery, the more likely that she would bear a low birth weight infant. Two more recent reports indicated that the birth

Table 1. Multiple Variables Affecting Perinatal Outcome

Maternal Age
  Chronologic
  Gynecologic
  Biologic

Demographic Factors
  Socioeconomic status
  Race
  Marital status
  Educational status
  Parity
  Geographic location
  Maternal height
  Maternal prepregnancy weight
  Maternal weight gain during pregnancy

Maternal Health Habits
  Compliance with and continuity of prenatal care
  Chronic or acute medical conditions
  Nutritional status
  Nutrition during pregnancy
  Substance abuse: smoking, alcohol, or drugs
  Urinary tract or cervical infections
  Third trimester coitus

---

weight of the infants of even very young adolescents can be changed by early and consistent prenatal care. McAnarney believes that even when the adolescent mother is under age 15, she should have no greater intrinsic likelihood of bearing a low birth weight infant than older adolescents or adults of similar backgrounds if she receives adequate prenatal care. This latter hypothesis warrants further investigation.

Psychosocial Risks of Early Childbearing

Adolescents who bear children are at risk psychologically and socially. Three major areas of consideration are maternal education, marriage, and welfare dependence.

Recent studies indicate that early childbearing is associated with significant educational losses for adolescent mothers. In one investigation, 50 percent of adolescent mothers received high school diplomas compared to 97 percent of women who still were not parents at 24 years of age.

The data reveal that 72 percent of adolescent marriages eventually terminate. Teenage marriages are generally unstable, regardless of the adolescent's age at the time of the birth of her first child. Thus, children of adolescent mothers are often reared in households headed by females.

Finally, there is a strong association between the receipt of welfare assistance and maternal age at the birth of the first child. This association diminishes when family size, education, and age at marriage are controlled.

Adolescent Mother-Infant Interaction

How do adolescent mothers differ from adult mothers? Studies show conflicting results. This is probably due to methodological difficulties, including confounding demographic variables and obtaining for study appropriate populations living under good conditions.

In 1979, McAnarney and her colleagues found that the younger the mother, the less she utilized synchrony, verbal communication, and closeness in her interaction with her infant. Although children of adolescent mothers appear to be as healthy as children of older mothers, little is known about their long-term socioemotional development. McAnarney and her colleagues are currently examining the data from their most recent study, which addresses this important issue.

The investigators videotaped 30 normal adolescent mothers and their normal infants in a laboratory setting during the first 3 postpartum days in two nonfeeding sequences of 10 minutes each, 24 hours apart. Nonfeeding sequences were used to permit varied interaction between mother and infant. Twelve adults served as a control group.

Maternal behaviors were observed and recorded in 15-second intervals according to the categories shown and defined in Table 2. The major infant category included crying or fussing, vocalizing, opening or closing eyes, and *en face* behaviors.

The data analysis compared maternal behaviors among early (12–14 years), middle (15–16 years), and late (17–20 years) adolescents for whom race, socioeconomic status, and marital status were similar. The results suggest that the adolescent mother at highest risk of parental dysfunction is a 15–16-year-old, non-black, lower-socioeconomic-status adolescent. Adolescent mothers in the middle age group received higher scores in the "assertive touch" category than both younger and older adolescents. The specific behaviors observed were "picking, poking, and pinching." During

Table 2. Seven Major Maternal Categories

Gentle Touch
Gentle exploration of the infant using finger touch; palmar hand stroking; kissing, gentle patting; embracing and fondling; and responding to the infant's behavior by attempting to calm him physically or emotionally in a gentle manner. Gentle jostling includes loving and warm playing.

Assertive Touch
Repetitive, assertive touching with fingertips (picking, poking, and pinching); or pushing, shoving, and shaking; abrupt and jerky movements.

Caretaking Behaviors
Any maternal behavior directed toward making the infant comfortable; for instance, straightening clothes, rewrapping the infant, or checking the diaper.

Proximity to Mother
Nearness in space of mother and infant; close contact or at least half of the infant's body touching the front of the mother's trunk.

Visual Behavior from Mother to Infant
Mother's eyes on infant: direct and prolonged glance; or *en face* behavior—mother orients her head into same plane as the infant, with eyes directed toward the infant's eyes.

Vocal or Verbal Behavior
Maternal vocalizations or verbalizations directed toward the infant.

Personal Behavior
Mother focuses on herself rather than on the infant; attends to combing her own hair, fixes her curlers, or reads and ignores her infant.

10-minute sessions the mean number of occurrences of these behaviors were 8.0, 13.8, and 4.2 for early, middle, and late adolescents, respectively. The mean for these picking, poking, and pinching behaviors for the same period of time was 0.17 for adults observed.

McAnarney feels that no firm conclusions may be drawn from these data at this point but that the display of such behaviors in middle adolescent mothers raises some interesting questions. Is such behavior related just to the age of the mother or to other variables, including race, socioeconomic status, and marital status? Are these behaviors predictive of future problems, like child abuse and neglect, poor compliance with well-child care, and poor developmental outcome for the child? Do these behaviors continue or drop out over time? Is it possible that the middle adolescent group suffers from the absence of a formal support system, perhaps more readily available to both younger and older groups?

Questions for Future Research

McAnarney believes that future research on adolescent mothers and their infants should address the following questions:

1. Which adolescent mother is at greatest risk for parenting her normal infant poorly?
2. What, if any, is the meaning of the picking, poking, and pinching behaviors observed in this study? Are these behaviors predictive of future morbidity, such as poor parenting?
3. Is there any reason to study early adolescent mother-infant interaction when the biological mother may have minimal responsibility for actually rearing her infant?
4. What is the socioemotional development of the children of adolescents as they mature?
5. Are there special parenting problems faced by the adolescent mother who rears a premature or sickly infant?

GROWING HAND IN HAND: INFANTS AND PARENTS AT RISK

Vivian Shapiro, M.S.W.

Introduction

Shapiro presents the preliminary findings of a clinical research study on psychologically impaired parents. Parents were rated on their psychological status, adequacy of physical and psychological caregiving, and modes of parent-child contact. Based on these ratings, parents were classified by degree of impairment. There was a positive relationship between psychological impairment of parents and the risk to the child. Improvement in children went hand in hand with improved parenting capacity.

Shapiro describes the design and preliminary findings of an exploratory investigation on psychologically impaired parents and their children. This clinical research study was undertaken at the Child Development Project (CDP) between 1972 and 1980. The research sample consisted of 50 infants and 41 families who were seen in treatment for six or more months. Shapiro notes that this number reflected the limit of CDP resources rather than the actual needs of the community. These families were generally distrubed and had a limited history of positive helping relationships. Disturbances were usually found in both the affective-social and adaptive development of the child and the parenting capacity of the mother and father. Specific child difficulties included failure to thrive, serious attachment disorders, and developmental irregularities. While most families were referred by physicians, social workers, and psychologists, some came of their own volition because of personal distress, depression, and marital discord. The 41 families were drawn from all socioeconomic levels, and ranged from professional couples to welfare recipients. As in many studies in this field, few fathers participated.

The assessment profile for these families included five areas. Four of these evaluated the child in terms of (1) health, (2) affective-social development, (3) adaptive development, and (4) cognitive development. The fifth area was the evaluation of parenting.

Evaluation of Parenting

The nature of the parent-child relationship was considered central to the evaluation of parenting. Gaining a proper understanding of this relationship required developing a positive working alliance with parents.

The basis for rating parental risk or impairment was the detailed parenting profile devised for this project. Shapiro lists the three major questions underlying this rating scale as follows:

1. Did the parent provide for the basic health, nutritional, and safety needs of the infant sufficiently to promote current and future health development?
2. Was a context for appropriate psychological and developmental growth of the child being provided?

3. Was the quality of the infant-parent relationship such as to promote the capacity for object relationships based on trust?

The profile itself included four areas: (1) psychological status of parents; (2) physical caregiving and nurturance; (3) psychological caregiving; and (4) quality of parent-child interaction.

Psychological Status of Parents. Parental status was described in the form of a brief history. The personality description highlighted the parents' competency, strengths, and vulnerabilities, specifically noting the affective status of the parent, characteristic modes of functioning, and coping and defense mechanisms.

Physical Caregiving and Nurturance. Meeting the basic safety and health needs of the child was the focus of this section of the profile. Criteria for evaluation included provision of adequate diet and nutrition, physical safety, basic hygiene, appropriate sleep routines, care during illness, and the use of appropriate health care judgment.

Psychological Caregiving. Psychological caregiving of the child was evaluated by rating the degree of support of the developing psychological self of the child in a phase-appropriate manner. This section included: the basic feeling-tone of the parent-child relationship; evidence of parental capacity to read and respond to the infant's signals; emotional availability and empathy, without undue distortion; knowledge of and support of developmental phases; and judgment in protecting the infant from undue stress or stimulation.

Quality of Parent-Child Interaction. Ratings in this section revealed the degree to which parents facilitated the development of reciprocal object relationships through their interactions with the child. Behaviors examined included: modes of contact and quality of contact—holding, gazing, talking, playing; the use of language and play in terms of form and content; and aversions or avoidance, or atypical modes of behavior.

Shapiro notes the importance of the relationship between the psychological status of the parent and the parent's ability to provide adequate physical and psychological care for the child in terms of nurturance, empathy, judgment, and parent-child interaction. In addition, the changing needs of the child call for adaptation on the part of the parent. Psychologically impaired parents often find it extremely difficult to make such adaptations.

Impairment Ratings of Parents

Parents in the clinical study were rated in each area on a scale from one to six, a continuum ranging from adequacy to critical impairment. Shapiro describes the key characteristics of those parents rated as critically, severely, seriously, and moderately impaired.

Critically Impaired Parents. This small group of parents showed the highest degree of impairment and dysfunction. These parents were experiencing such a high level of psychological disorganization that they could provide next to no care for themselves or their children. Key characteristics included: inability to provide for basic needs of the infant or to assess the infant's major life-needs realistically; inability to empathize; projection of distorted and negative images onto the infant; critical lack of knowledge about children; and impaired or absent judgment or worry.

The CDP data showed that children in these extremely dysfunctional families already showed signs of impairment in all four areas of development—health, cognition, affect, and adaptive functioning. These children were often abused or neglected. The social isolation of such families made community support very difficult to provide.

A rating of "critical impairment" implied a clinical judgment that intensive outreach services would not be sufficient to reach the parent in time to save the infant from immediate harm. Placement, hospitalization, or protective care of the child was deemed urgent.

Severely Impaired Parents. This larger group of parents had both personal and psychological difficulties and impairment in caregiving. The infants of these parents were obviously at risk in the adaptive and affective areas of development, as well as in terms of their health. However, they were not necessarily imminently at risk, as in the case of the infants of critically impaired parents.

Infants in this group were referred because of serious concerns, including failure to thrive, threat of abuse, the existence of neglect, and obvious developmental difficulties. Extensive active outreach seemed warranted in these families, and all efforts were made to develop a working alliance with the parents. However, there was great difficulty in establishing a working alliance with these parents because of their lack of basic trust. Many of them lacked a history of helping supportive individuals as well as any personal experience to indicate that life could get better. When a close positive alliance could be formed, the infant's developmental needs usually led the way to the therapeutic work on parental behavior.

Histories of the severely impaired parents revealed traumatic, painful childhoods, much like the lives of their own children. In all cases, the infants of these parents evoked old unresolved conflicts. This would make the infant the target of distorted images and dysfunctional care.

Some of the statements made about their infants by severely impaired parents included serious distortions and fears. The infant obviously represented another self or a different time and place. Despite the transference difficulties, the parents were able to form a treatment alliance.

Seriously Impaired Parents. As compared with the groups of parents described up to this point, seriously impaired parents showed better ego integration or a better sense of self and others, which enabled them to respond to the infant as a changing, evolving person. Although impaired, there was a greater differentiation between the parent's own needs and the child's needs, a more appropriate use of information, the ability to seek information without distortion, and generally less serious global parental disturbance.

The problems of this group were significant, but the infant was not as firmly enmeshed in the center of parental pathology as in the more disturbed parents. Treatment was indicated, and the clinician expressed significant concern for the future of the family and the parent-child relationship; however, the infant was safeguarded to some degree.

Shapiro provides brief highlights of case histories to clarify the dimensions of this category.

> ...an infant was born with a cleft palate to parents who had their own history of unattended medical illness and early trauma. This birth, their second child, created a crisis situation for the parents which seemed to immobilize them. The mother and father literally could not face their infant or help her through the painful medical procedures. When this infant was first seen at the CDP, she was significantly retarded, primarily because of a lack of attention and care. The parents could not deal with their own

anxiety and could not give comfort to their own infant without help. As treatment began, the infant improved dramatically.

...an infant was born to a young mother whose own parents had survived the Holocaust. Unexpectedly, this mother became exceedingly anxious. She alternated between being very harsh with her child to being overwhelmed by guilt, sorrow, and anxiety to the point of inaction. The birth of the infant had re-evoked memories and sorrow of the past that had long been forgotten.

...depression followed the birth of the infant. The depression was related to complex childhood events which included abandonment by an ill mother. This new mother wanted to protect her infant and was able to make sure that it was cared for, but she, herself, could not relate to it at this time of crisis.

In all of these cases, as maternal depression was understood, parenting became more spontaneous and the infants' development improved.

Moderately Impaired Parents. These parents showed a higher and more stable level of parental functioning than the three previous groups. There was more evidence of a normal range of parental adaptive capacity, more reality in the assessment and responsiveness to the needs of the infant, more joy and a wider range of parental expression of feelings, and more awareness of the difficulties they were facing as parents. Frequently these parents had difficulties with specific developmental issues and requested guidance and support. In some cases the infants had special caregiving needs, such as early illness, placing extra stress on the parents.

Moderately impaired parents took a more active role in monitoring their own behavior and their child's development, even though they had difficulty in some areas. Shapiro notes that more than half the parents who started in the study with a rating of seriously impaired improved to the degree of moderate impairment. This is an important finding because it underscores the point made by other investigators in the field that parenting can improve through appropriate interventions.

Conclusions of the Study

Preliminary findings indicate that three conclusions can be drawn. The first is that environmental as well as physical considerations can place an infant at risk developmentally. The second is that the degree of psychological impairment of the parent constitutes the risk status of the child. The third conclusion is that improvement in infants goes hand in hand with improved parental well-being and parenting ability.

The data lend strong support to the self-righting tendencies of organisms described by Sameroff and others. In the present study, over 80 percent of the infants made some improvement toward adequacy, as did at least one of the parents of each.

Finally, this study has implications for treatment. Shapiro points out that methods of treatment need to account not only for infant needs but also for parental needs. Developing a working alliance with parents who need help is a difficult task. It requires perserverance and commitment on the part of health-care providers.

PARENTS OF MEDICALLY IMPAIRED INFANTS

Carolyn R. Aradine, R.N., Ph.D.

Introduction

Aradine examines the impact of chronic health problems of an infant on parenting and family relationships. She presents findings from her research on medically impaired infants whose respiratory problems required long-term tracheostomies. This type of medical problem can have serious consequences for the infant's development, the parents' behavior, and the functioning of the family as a unit.

Parents of medically impaired infants are at risk for dysfunction because of the enormous stresses placed on them and the difficult adjustments required of them. The literature suggests that an infant's chronic health problems affect parenting and family functioning. Specifically, consequences may include extreme emotional reactions by parents, lack of acceptance of child or of situation, incomplete mourning, feelings of helplessness and lack of control, economic burdens, suboptimal parenting behavior, and additional medical problems. These parents also show high incidences of separation and divorce.

Most studies of families with chronically ill children report data collected from mothers, with few direct reports by fathers. Existing research on fathers indicates that fathers have less contact with health professionals than mothers, but fathers feel that both parents need professional contact and support. They reported intense feelings about the child's diagnosis, but many felt at the same time responsible to support their wives. Many fathers found their career mobility limited by the ill or handicapped child and also experienced marital discord, diminished leisure activities, health problems, and preoccupation and concern for their wives and children. Although areas of impact are generally agreed upon, predicting and facilitating a family's successful coping with such problems are less well clarified.

Infants with Long-Term Tracheostomies

Little data exist on the impact of home care of a child with a tracheostomy. Recent research suggests that parents of such children need detailed instructions and continuing support from health professionals. These parents worry about hearing the infant at night or leaving him with a babysitter. Disturbances in relationships may develop between the parents and the affected child and between themselves. Parents may become controlling, anxious, intrusive, and inconsistent about discipline.

In the present study, Aradine investigated further the impact of long-term tracheostomy on the infant, his or her development, and the parents. She studied five infants who had required long-term tracheostomies to relieve an airway obstruction due to glottic or subglottic stenosis. The families were visited and interviewed at home four to six times over a six-week period. All families who participated were intact; four of the families had more than one child. Interviews were open-ended. Three couples participated together; two mothers participated without their husbands. In addition to the interviews, parents were observed with their children, and the children's developmental progress was monitored through Bayley assessment and videotaped play observations.

A major focus of the study was the emotional and behavioral reactions of the parents to caring for an infant with this severe medical problem. In the interview situations, parents described in detail their concerns about the child's care, necessary family adjustments, and their isolation from outside social activities. All parents indicated their desire for ongoing professional guidance and support. Aradine describes the parents' initial reactions in the hospital setting, the stresses experienced after bringing the child home, and long-term follow-up.

Parents' Initial Reactions

Aradine describes all the parents as "shocked, terrified, and anxious" as they watched their infants struggle to breathe and were told of the necessity of tracheostomy. All feared that the child would die. Some of the infants were premature; others needed emergency surgery and had to be rushed from home to the hospital. Some of the infants refused to look at the mother, refused to eat, and showed vigorous resistance and head-banging. These behaviors were very difficult for the parents to witness.

Discharge was arranged after all the parents were prepared by the hospital staff to care for their infants at home. Parents practiced and familiarized themselves with important procedures while the infants were still in the hospital. The transition from hospital to home setting was perceived as difficult by the parents, and many mixed emotions and worries were triggered at this point in the crisis. The joy was tempered by fear and anxiety.

Fear took the form of worrying about all the things that could possibly go wrong. In particular, parents feared that they would not be able to hear the infant, who could not cry to signal distress, especially at night when they would be sleeping. They also worried that the child might experience complications at home, for example, infections, dislodged tracheostomy tube, mucous plugs, or respiratory distress, requiring rehospitalization. They worried about being inadequate caregivers and about the use of specific techniques and equipment. They were also concerned that they would not get everything done or that their older children or someone else might inadvertently harm the infant.

Stresses Experienced with the Infant at Home

Aradine describes the stresses and exhaustion experienced by parents caring for their medically impaired infants. Infants with tracheostomies require a great deal of time-consuming and exacting physical care in addition to the normal activities of infant care. This special care includes frequent suctioning, humidification of the airway, changing tracheostomy-tube ties and pads and sometimes the tubes themselves, postural drainage, cleaning and care of the equipment, and protection of the airway.

After about one week at home, the parents became more comfortable with these procedures, as they learned that they could provide care successfully. They also learned to recognize infant signals of distress other than crying, such as movements or changes in breathing. However, their ongoing concerns reflected the continuing impact of the child's medical problems on the parents.

All parents emphasized the need for constant surveillance, keeping the child in visual or auditory range. At night, most children slept in their parents' bedrooms to reduce the parents' fears that they would not know if their child suddenly needed them.

Getting everything done for the infant and for the family produced great stress and pressure. Adjusting to a new and demanding routine was difficult and created strain in the home. So much time and energy had to be devoted to the medically impaired child that other activities were neglected, and there was little time for play or leisure. Social activity, recreation, and vacations were reduced. Even relatives were seen far less frequently, partly because of time constraints and partly due to fear of potential illness or discomfort for the child. The isolation and confinement added to the stress of the situation.

All of these fears, guilts, time constraints, and difficult adjustments placed stress on the parents' marriage. The inability to relax and enjoy life made it almost impossible to carry on normal sexual relations.

In addition to the physical and psychological stresses of this crisis, the parents voiced two vehement complaints about the health services they received: conflicting advice and impersonal service. They appreciated the opportunity to talk about their experience, and they longed for answers to their questions and the opportunity to talk with someone who understood their situation. When Aradine offered to continue to work with the families, four of the five accepted her help.

Long-Term Follow-Up

Aradine underscores the need for long-term data on families with medically impaired infants. It is crucial to examine the physical and psychological risks for the child as it grows older. Unfortunately, there is little data on the long-range impact of this chronic medical condition on later development or on the family.

In the present study, long-term follow-up—for as long as four years—involved weekly visits with two families, biweekly to monthly visits with the third family, and periodic visits (every one to three months) with the fourth. Both mothers and fathers participated. Aradine provided the nursing care and kept detailed progress notes of the visits. The nursing care included: health guidance, developmental guidance, emotional support and counseling, specific interventions related to special individual problems, guidance and intervention in dealing with the complex health-care systems, and coordination of services with other professionals.

The progress notes pinpointed a variety of concerns. With each crisis, old worries and fears were triggered, and uncertainties about the child's treatment arose. Although the families learned to master the health system, it was never easy for them. In addition, two of the five sets of parents divorced during the next two years. One couple divorced soon after the child's tracheostomy tube was removed and the other when the child was about four years of age after the medical problems had been resolved.

In all cases, parents' concerns for the child increased immediately after the tracheostomy tube was removed. This transition was far more traumatic for the parents than the health professionals had expected. Parents worried at this time about croup, colds, pneumonia, respiratory arrest, and whether the child would require another tracheostomy. Confidence was gained as the post-tracheostomy period became stabilized.

Implications

More is known about the difficulties experienced by families with chronically ill or handicapped infants and children as this important area becomes more of a focus for research. However, there is little information about effective strategies and interventions that health professionals can apply during this period of crisis. Aradine believes that the potential for effective and ongoing nursing care for such families is greater than their current utilization. She believes that specialized training for health care professionals who work with parents of medically impaired children is necessary to reduce the risk of dysfunction.

PARENTS WHO HAVE LOST A CHILD BY DEATH

Sherry Johnson-Soderberg, R.N., Ph.D.

Introduction

Johnson-Soderberg analyzes the complexities of guilt and its impact on grief after the loss of a child by death. In her study of 14 couples, Johnson-Soderberg explores the manifestations of different types of guilt in thoughts and behavior of parents and examines the mediating influence of short versus long preparation time for the crisis. The need for more research and effective intervention to reduce the risk for these parents is emphasized.

The death of a child is a catastrophic event for a family. It may evoke strong feelings of guilt in parents. Johnson-Soderberg believes that guilt is a common, complicated, and often misunderstood variable in the mourning process. The guilt that results from grief may be related to the high divorce rate of parents who have lost a child by death. Because of its negative impact, it is important for health professionals to examine this factor carefully as a first step toward preventing, treating, and resolving guilt behavior in these parents.

In her review of the literature, Johnson-Soderberg examines the origins of guilt in the developmental process and sexual differences in the expression of guilt. Guilt is a learned behavior that results from an awareness of (1) others as separate beings, (2) the possibility of having empathic responses to the feelings of others, and (3) having a responsibility for the feelings or situations of others. The guilty feelings may be derogatory feelings toward another person or toward oneself. Research indicates that women are more expressive than men concerning guilt, probably as a result of the sex-role socialization process. Factors such as the affective atmosphere of the home, role modeling of the parents, cultural and religious beliefs, age, experiences, and the method of transmission of parental values and beliefs all contribute to the quality and intensity in the development of guilt.

There has been little research on guilt as it relates to the processes of grieving and mourning. Reported case studies indicate that guilt reactions frequently accompany mourning and can have a strong impact on the mourner's adjustment to the death of a loved one. To clarify the nature and impact of guilt, Johnson-Soderberg has broken down this complex construct into logical components.

Types of Guilt

Johnson-Soderberg identifies three major types of guilt: personal, existential, and anticipatory. *Personal guilt* is the result of an act of commission (action) or omission (inaction). Commission is the earliest form of guilt that develops. It occurs when the child's empathic response and the awareness of harming another occur together (e.g., parent points out to the child that it is not appropriate to hit another person). Omission occurs when the child gains the ability to think abstractly of an event that might have occurred but did not. For example, the child may be blamed for the continuation of another person's distress because he or she did not act in a way that would decrease the distress.

Existential guilt occurs when a person feels culpable because of circumstances in life that are beyond his or her control. The definition of existential guilt incorporates the involvement of social and ethical situations that conflict with values or ethical positions. There are three necessary conditions for existential guilt: (1) identification with another person's plight, (2) conscious feelings of being at an advantage, and (3) feeling helpless to change a situation.

Anticipatory guilt occurs when a person has the capacity to predict an act of commission or omission; it is a fantasized potential. This type of guilt is more often a basis for future decision-making than a measure of present guilt intensity.

The first type of guilt described—personal guilt—may be unimagined or imagined, humanistic or conventional, and self-grounded or other-grounded. These components of personal guilt are illustrated in Figure 1. *Unimagined guilt* occurs when the person believes that he or she has committed an actual wrong-doing either commission or omission to oneself or to another. This event could be in the past or present. *Imagined guilt* is the result of fantasizing an act of omission or commission to oneself or to another. The fantasy occurs in the past or present. *Self-grounded guilt* occurs when an act of commission or omission is committed against oneself. *Other-grounded guilt* involves committing an act of commission or omission against another person.

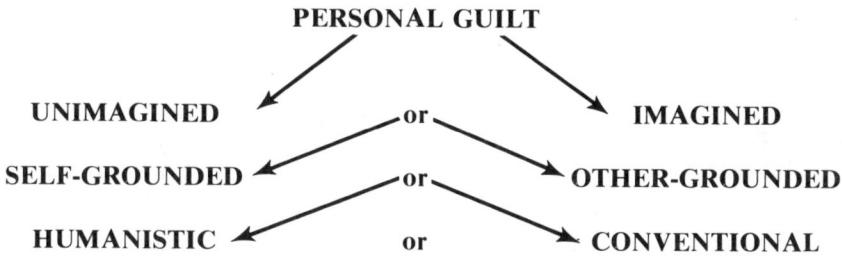

Figure 1. Components of personal guilt.

Humanistic guilt is based on any act that causes harm to oneself or another with the resulting feeling of guilt (e.g., a hit-and-run accident). *Conventional guilt* is the result of a deviation from a social norm ("you should not get pregnant before marriage"), role expectations ("mothers should stay home and take care of children, and fathers should work"), and cultural conventions ("little children should not play with matches").

Personal guilt may be imagined or unimagined. Personal, uniagined guilt may be self-grounded and humanistic, other-grounded and humanistic, self-grounded and conventional, or other-grounded and conventional. Personal, imagined guilt may be divided in the same fashion.

Unlike personal guilt, anticipatory guilt can only be imagined, since it concerns predicting future feelings based on potential future events. Like personal guilt, anticipatory guilt may be self-grounded or other-grounded, humanistic or conventional.

Study on Parents Who Have Lost a Child by Death

The purpose of this survey was to identify the presence or absence of guilt, number of guilt statements, and types of guilt experienced by parents who lost a child by death. This study examined associations among the length of preparation time for death, demographic data, and specific guilt behaviors.

Data was systematically collected from the designated population by semi-structured interviews, a self-administered questionnaire, and scales. Parents whose child had died were asked to recall experiences and feelings before the child became ill, during the illness, and after the death but within the first year of bereavement. Their guilt-related statements were classified according to the categories described above and related to characteristics of the population.

The 28 individuals (14 couples) who participated were white, middle-class parents who had experienced the death of a child within the year prior to the initial interview but at least six weeks after the death. Homicides, natural disasters, stillbirths, and suicides were excluded from the study. Death was a result of terminal illness, accident, or sudden infant death syndrome (SIDS). The dead children were between 9 days and 13 years of age, with a mean age of 2.9 years. The mothers' ages ranged from 24 to 48 years, with a mean age of 31.7 years. The fathers' ages ranged from 26 to 53 years, with a mean age of 33.8 years.

A total of 451 statements of guilt were made. These were divided by sex and preparation time for the death (Table 3). Parents in the short-preparation group expressed many more guilt statements than those in the long-preparation group; women in both groups expressed significantly ($t = 2.46$, $P = 0.02$) more guilt statements than did men.

Table 3. Total Guilt Statements

Group	Women	Men	Total
SPG (No. = 16)*	207	120	327
LPG (No. = 12)†	83	41	124

* SPG = short-preparation group (under two weeks to prepare).
† LPG = long-preparation group (15 days or more to prepare).

The most frequent types of guilt for the short-preparation group were personal, unimagined, self-grounded, and conventional (55); and personal, unimagined, other-grounded, and conventional (55). The most frequent types of guilt for the long-preparation group were personal, unimagined, other-grounded, and conventional; (34) and personal, unimagined, other-grounded, and humanistic (29).

In addition to the guilt diagnosis of statements, 12 guilt themes emerged:

1. parenting
2. God/punishing
3. pregnancy
4. cemetary visiting
5. hindering people, including guilt instillers
6. movies
7. circumstances
8. saying good-bye, relief, terminating, and funeral
9. expressing another's guilt
10. grieving
11. sex
12. general guilt

The experience of "movie" scenes, or compulsive and intrusive negative images, about the death of the child seemed to reinforce the guilt. One participant describes the "movies" in this way:

> It is a kind of a repetitive thought, like a nightmare, only you are not asleep. It occurs just during waking hours when you are obsessed by one thought or one feeling, like some drama is being played out in your head over and over again. There is no escaping it.

In all cases, the "movie" was connected to frequent and intense guilt. In the short-preparation group the "movies" dealt with the death scene. In the long-preparation group a woman's "movie" occurred the night before her child died:

> Well, I had the experience in the hospital the night before surgery. Annie wanted me to stay with her all night, but I

said that I would stay with her until she fell asleep at which point I would go back to the nurses' quarters to sleep. She wanted me to stay with her and I should have (crying very hard). I did not sleep, so I do not know why I just did not stay in her room. I feel terrible guilt over that—just terrible.

For both the long- and short-preparation groups, secret guilt "movies" are very potent reminders of the deaths that seem to torture these people. The short-preparation group reported having more "movies" than the long-preparation group. For those who had such "movies," they mentioned that sharing these experiences during the study, which was an emotional experience for them, was a great relief. Often it was the first time that they shared these experiences with anyone. These torturing "movies" had led them to believe they were going crazy until they realized that other parents in their situation were having similar experiences.

When asked to define feelings of guilt, the responses were very personal and individualized and produced a variety of reactions and feelings, including depression and worthlessness.

The short- and long-preparation groups found different ways to alleviate their guilt. The short-preparation group used talking, information, physical activities, or drinking to alleviate guilt. The long-preparation group used talking, "mind control," time, and undoing.

Eighty-one percent of the short-preparation group and ninety-two percent of the long-preparation group could describe the circumstances that led them to decide to live again. For both groups, the reasons revolved around work, family, and a replacement child.

Johnson-Soderberg discusses the issue of "replacement children" and how this decision establishes a new goal for the couple, filling a void and undoing the guilt. But are these replacement children at risk? In the short-preparation group, three couples have had a child within the first year of bereavement and two are presently pregnant. In the long-preparation group only one mother was of childbearing age, and she had physical problems and was advised not to become pregnant. Of the eleven couples in the study who are of childbearing age, three have had babies, three are pregnant, two have physical problems, two are undecided, and one has a newborn. Of these 11 couples, 55 percent had a child or were pregnant within the first year of bereavement. Although these couples believed they could not "replace" their dead child, they wanted another child of the same sex as quickly as possible.

Questions that emerge are: What is the effect of the parents' guilt on the new child? Is it pathological to have a "replacement" child? How do parents who are no longer of childbearing years replace their loss?

Johnson-Soderberg believes that this study is a preliminary step toward the development of nursing theory about parental guilt and that effective intervention strategies will be designed based on this theory. She underscores the need for further research in this area to reduce the risk for parents who have lost a child by death.

PARENTS OF THE PREMATURE INFANT

Suzanne Hall Johnson, R.N., M.N.

Introduction

Johnson describes the stresses on parents of premature infants, their special emotional and practical problems, and useful professional strategies for alleviating some of these difficulties. These stresses and problems include: unpreparedness, transport, intensive-care environment, behavior of the premature infant, guilt, blame, anger, grief, exhaustion, role changes, and multiple crises. It is important that health-care professionals be alert to these stresses and learn how to intervene effectively.

The birth of a premature infant is a very stressful event for most parents. The couple is unprepared not only for the birth itself, but also for the critical-care environment in which their infant is placed. The violation of their expectations for a normal child, the fear of the unknown, and other personal difficulties all place pressure on the parents of the premature infant. Such pressures put these parents at risk for marital dysfunction and dysfunction in their relationship with their child.

Stresses Related to Premature Birth

The parents of premature infants undergo a variety of stresses related to both medical and environmental changes. Johnson believes that the major stress factors are: unpreparedness, infant transport, intensive-care environment, facing the unknown, and unexpected infant behavior.

Because in most cases parents of a premature infant expected the pregnancy to go full-term, they are unprepared for the delivery. They may not have completed childbirth education classes and may not have selected the hospital in which to give birth. The stress of unpreparedness can have a negative impact on labor and the delivery process, putting both mother and child at risk.

In the case of a premature infant born in a rural or isolated geographical area, special transport to a main medical center for intensive care may be required. Although many mothers are transported before delivery in a risk situation, many premature births are unexpected, and the mother may deliver in the rural hospital. In such situations, the child may be transported separately to the regional medical center. This separation from the newborn causes increased stress for the parents, who may consider it an extreme measure. They may even fear for the child's life.

Additional stress is often created by both the realities and fantasies of the intensive-care environment. Johnson believes that this environment often causes the parents' great stress. It is uncomfortable, noisy, and impersonal, and most parents are unprepared for it. It taps their fears of the unknown in the same way as the transport of their infant. The less prepared the parents are for these events, the more stress they will undergo.

Another source of stress, also related to being unprepared and faced with the unknown, involves the behavior of the premature infant. Unlike the full-term infant, the premature infant has premature reflexes and behaviors. For example, it may not grasp as strongly or smile as readily as the full-term infant. Parents are often concerned when their infant does not respond in the ways in which they anticipated. They may misinterpret this as dislike or disapproval. The premature infant's weak suck can be misinterpreted by the parents as their inability to feed and care for their child. These misconceptions can have a negative impact on their parenting and consequently on the child's behavior and emotional state. This can be a very self-defeating cycle.

In addition to these stresses, the parents encounter other problems. Johnson identified them through a content analysis of responses of 212 parents of premature infants. One major problem is the experience of grief; others include overcoming guilt and exhaustion and dealing with multiple crises, role changes, and discipline.

Many parents of premature infants tend to blame themselves for the early birth. They feel that they did something wrong or neglected to do something important. Some parents blame each other or other people—for example, the health professional most closely involved with them.

Most parents experience grief following a premature birth. They grieve not only over the loss of a "normal child" but also over the loss of the opportunity to be a "normal parent." They miss showing the child to friends and family members, being able to breast-feed immediately, and other processes associated with normal parenting.

Another major problem for these parents is exhaustion. This is a problem for parents under ordinary circumstances, but it is compounded in the case of prematurity. Handling the new stresses, visiting the child, taking care of the rest of the family, and going to work are responsibilities that can be exhausting during this crisis period.

The crisis of the premature birth triggers multiple crises for the parents. The immediate crisis of the first 24 hours is the fear that the child might die. When the child is released from the hospital and the parents become the primary caregivers, they may fear that the child will die in their care. The parents, living in fear, find any daily experience seems like a crisis and adds stress.

In addition, difficulties can result from the disappointments of unfulfilled expectations. The husband and wife may feel let down by one another or by their premature child. They may experience the stresses of having to change roles and take on roles with which they feel uncomfortable. Johnson found this to be a problem even a year or two following a premature birth.

Lack of discipline is another problem that arises. Frequently these parents want to help the child "catch up," not only in weight but also in love. Permissiveness is sometimes carried to such an extent that the child receives anything he or she wants and learns how to manipulate the family, which can cause even more stress.

Strategies for Professionals

Johnson describes six strategies that can be used by members of the health team to help reduce the stress of a premature birth on the parents. The health team may include the physician, nurse, physical therapist, dietitian, social worker, psychologist, or others, and these strategies can be mastered and applied effectively by any of these professionals. The strategies are as follows:

1. *Avoid False Rescuing Behaviors.* Giving false hope or empty encouragement does not help parents in this situation nor does it help to alleviate their grief and pain. Such ineffectual rescuing statements include, "Your child will turn out alright, it is just going to take time."
2. *Increase Interaction with Infant.* Increased intimacy and interaction with the infant allows the parent to take on their normal role. Johnson believes that it is up to the professionals to encourage not only eye-to-eye contact and touching but also stroking. This contact helps allay parents' fears about the infants' behavior and their own performance.
3. *Encourage Appropriate Role Shifts.* When the parents' roles are complementary, they can help each other in the crisis situation of premature birth. However, when their roles are in conflict (e.g., if one assumes all the responsibility for visiting and care) or confused, the crisis can escalate. Johnson believes that health professionals can help parents to shift their roles more smoothly and work together more productively in meeting the difficult day-to-day responsibilities.
4. *Give Parents More Control.* A central theme in the stresses suffered by parents of premature infants is their lack of control in the hospital situation. Health professionals can give parents more control and thus alleviate some of their stress by allowing them to decide on such matters as visiting time, feeding time, and discharge date. Assistance in making such decisions may be provided when it is requested or needed.
5. *Avoid Assumptions of What Is Best for Parents.* It is important for health professionals to keep in mind that every parent reacts uniquely to the crisis of premature birth. A statement that is comforting to one mother might be painful to another mother. A useful suggestion for one father might provoke resentment or anger in another father. Sensitivity to these differences and flex-

ibility in providing what is needed in each case are useful skills for health-care professionals.

6. *Increase the Parents' Pride in Their Infant.* Part of the role of the health-care professional is to help the parents to be proud of their new infant. Pointing out their infants' strengths will help the parents appreciate the uniqueness and complexity of their child. They will learn to see him or her as a strong human being with a promising future.

WHEN THE INJURY IS A SYMPTOM: INTERRELATIONS AMONG THE PEDIATRIC SOCIAL ILLNESSES

Eli H. Newberger, M.D.[1]

Introduction

Newberger presents clinical and research data on the origins and consequences of pediatric social illnesses, with a focus on child abuse. Departing from a medical one-to-one philosophy of cause and effect, a model that cannot be applied to complex social issues, Newberger's research takes a multitude of variables and cases into account. Paths to the pediatric social illnesses and a profile of high-risk families are described.

The diagnosis of social illnesses by means of a medical one-to-one cause-and-effect model results in oversimplification and distortion of the many complex issues involved. Child abuse, rather than being a diagnosis, is a symptom that indicates a distraught parent and a

---

[1] The studies described herein, were conducted by Dr. Newberger in collaboration with Thomas J. Marx, Ed.D., and were supported by National Institute of Mental Health Grant No. 1 T0 1551701A2CD.

troubled family. The parents as well as the children show many patterns of risk. There is no one single familial configuration that corresponds to and causes a given pediatric social illness. This open philosophy of cause and effect asserts that an effect may have several sets of causes or that a single set of causes may lead to several effects. Newberger believes that this philosophy is more realistic than a medical philosophy for the design of better treatment and prevention programs for families with pediatric social illnesses. Eventually, treatment will be directed toward overcoming the social, psychological, and economic weaknesses of the targeted family configurations and using their strengths productively. Newberger presents clinical observations and research data to support the open-philosophy model.

Strain Equals Stress Minus Strength

In the first of a series of studies, interviews were conducted over a period of two years to compile data on 506 families with children under age four years admitted to Children's Hospital Medical Center in Boston. It was hypothesized that strain, defined as the excess of past and present stress over self-strength, in the mother or caretaker was the cause of the four types of pediatric social illness in this study—failure to thrive, abuse, ingestion, and accident. It was predicted that a caretaker's self-perceived strength would act as a counterbalance against the occurrence of pediatric social illness even where stress in the caretaker was high. In this equation, strain equals stress minus strength.

A Profile of High-Risk Families

In a later phase of this series a sample consisting of 418 matched cases and controls divided into four pediatric social illnesses and four matched control groups was examined. The illnesses considered were abuse, failure to thrive, ingestion, and accident. A structured interview was given to the patient's mother at the hospital after the diagnosis had been made. Areas covered in the interview were: mother's childhood; mother's educational and occupational attainments; mother's present relationship with the child, a man, and kin; mother's state of mind; father's background as reported by the mother; child's development, health, and state of mind as seen by the mother; and family economic circumstances, housing, and mobility.

Too few fathers participated for their interviews to be included in the analysis.

In support of the findings from the first phase of this investigation, there was a strong resemblance between abuse and failure-to-thrive families. There was a general trend for abused children to exhibit poor physical growth which, when sufficiently extreme, could classify a child as failure to thrive. The implication for treatment of the family—as opposed to treatment of the child—is that focus on the injury or condition may be a distraction. Newberger believes the search should be for particular patterns of family function and treatments rather than simplified labels and diagnoses.

In the full sample of 418 families, 48 (11 percent) were diagnosed as abusive. In the high-risk group about three times that number (35 percent) were classified as abusive. In contrast, the low and lowest risk groups had 7 percent and 4 percent of their respective totals in the abusive category.

What are the characteristics of high-risk families? Newberger provides a preliminary profile in nine vital aspects of their lives.

1. *Mother's Childhood.* The parents of mothers in high-risk families often disagreed about child-rearing, according to the mother. These mothers remembered being disciplined more severely than mothers in the low-risk groups. High-risk mothers were more often hit with objects, as well as on parts of the body than hands or buttocks. For many of them, physical discipline continued into adolescence. High-risk mothers rated their childhoods as "neutral," in contrast to low-risk mothers who felt they were "somewhat happy" as children.
2. *Mother's Attainments.* The more responsible the mother's occupation, the less risk of her child being abused or undernourished. From the highest to lowest risk, mothers' occupations were: unskilled or semiskilled labor, skilled labor, and clerical work. The same pattern held for education. In high-risk families, mothers had rarely completed high school; mothers in low-risk families were either high school graduates or had had some college education.
3. *Father's Background.* Whereas most fathers in high-risk families were raised in rural locations, most fathers in the low-risk groups were raised in urban locations. There was also a slightly higher rate of broken marriages among parents of fathers in high-risk families.

4. *Family Wealth.* High-risk families were poor. Their earning power was about half of that of low-risk families. There were a greater number of high-risk than low-risk families on welfare.
5. *Mother's State.* High-risk mothers voiced more health complaints than low-risk mothers. Coupled with health problems, many high-risk mothers found it hard to "get going" in the morning and watched about 7½ hours of television per day (twice as much as low-risk mothers). High-risk mothers generally had fewer support systems or friends than their low-risk counterparts.
6. *Mother and Men.* In almost all high-risk families, mothers were single, separated, or divorced. In low-risk families, about half the mothers were married; the others were divorced or separated. In the low-risk families, almost all mothers were married. In addition, high-risk mothers had less stable relationships. In these homes, there was either no man or a temporary or occasional man.
7. *Mother and Kin.* Relating with kin was the only aspect of the lives of high-risk mothers not deficient relative to the low-risk groups. All mothers visited their relatives and wanted to see them more often.
8. *Mother and Child.* High-risk mothers found their children more difficult to manage than low-risk mothers. However, they did not report more spanking than the low-risk groups.
9. *Child's State.* The data on the child's state came from the mother's impressions after the child's admission to the hospital. Newberger cautions that the mother's interview might be colored by her reactions to health professionals who conferred with her. High-risk mothers appraised their child's usual health as between fair and good. Mothers in the two low-risk groups described their children's health as good to excellent.

Newberger concludes that whether or not abuse or undernourishment has occurred in these high-risk families, they usually have great difficulty maintaining intimate relationships and usually have inadequate financial means. The mother's entire life has often been lived in poverty, punctuated by violence and abandonment. Realistically, each patient requires years of assistance and counseling. This need is rarely met. Like so many other investigators in the field, Newberger underscores the necessity for more research so that appropriate intervention strategies may be developed.

STAGES OF PARENTAL UNDERSTANDING IN CHILD ABUSE AND NEGLECT

Carolyn Moore Newberger, Ed.D.[1]

Introduction

Newberger and Cook investigate the relationship between level of parental reasoning and degree of parental dysfunction as reflected in child abuse and neglect. Four levels of parental conceptions concerning the child, child-rearing, and parenting are identified. In order of increasing complexity, these levels are: egoistic, conventional, individualistic, and analytic. A manual with examples and criteria for each cognitive level has been developed from this research data.

Carolyn Newberger examines the cognitive dimensions of parenthood and the relationship between parental reasoning and parental adaptation to the stresses and demands of child-rearing. The parent's conceptions of the child and of the parental role seem logically to represent cognitive structure in parenthood. Cognitive structure refers to stable patterns of thought that define how an individual makes sense out of experience and organizes his or her responses to it. As applied to parenthood, cognitive structure might be revealed in the organization of reasoning about the child's experiences, the effects of experience on the child, and justice and responsibility in the parental role.

In her research, Newberger studies parental awareness, which she defines as the development of understanding children and the tasks of becoming a parent and raising a child. Parental awareness can be thought of as an organized knowledge system with which the parent makes sense out of the child's responses and behavior and formulates policies to guide parental action. At successive stages of parental awareness, parents would be aware of deeper aspects of the child and

---

[1] The studies described herein were conducted by D. Carolyn Newberger in collaboration with Susan J. Cook, M.A.

of more complex interactions between the child and themselves. With greater awareness, greater flexibility evolves in sorting through the dimensions and arriving at resolutions of the tasks of parenthood. Newberger points out that parental awareness differs from parental attitudes in that the former deals with the underlying structure of concepts about people and relationships, whereas the latter deals with points of view and opinions, which are more subject to change.

Levels of Parental Awareness

In Newberger's investigation of levels of parental awareness, 51 parents from a broad cross section of social and familial backgrounds were interviewed. These parents were selected from an outpatient clinic at a large urban pediatric hospital and from neighboring middle-class suburbs.

The issues addressed in the semistructured parental awareness interview included: (1) conceptions of the child (influences on the child's development, subjective experience of the child, conception of the ideal child, and personality of the child); (2) conceptions of child-rearing (meaning of communication and trust, function and role of discipline and authority, methods and reasons for conflict resolution, and defining, assessing, and meeting the needs of the child); and (3) conceptions of the parental role (learning and evaluating parenting).

Four types of cognitive structures, or levels of parental awareness, emerged from a content analysis of these interviews. Each structure, stage, or level was self-consistent, forming a cohesive whole and influencing how the parent conceptualized child-rearing across a number of issues. These four levels are organized in a developmental hierarchy analogous to Piaget's stages of cognitive development. The four levels of parental awareness are: egoistic, conventional, individualistic, and analytic.

Level 1—Egoistic. At level 1, parents interpret the child and his experiences through the narrow lens of the parents' sense of self-need, desire, and projections. The parental role becomes organized around fulfilling these personal needs and desires. The process of defining the needs of the child is described more in terms of the parents' specific actions than in the child's experience of that action. The parents at this level may focus on the effort made, as proof of their ability to respond to the child, rather than on the nature of what they do and its effect on the child. The egocentricity at this level may be further reflected by the parents' focus on the behavior of the child that specifically causes discomfort for the parents. Thus, at level 1 of parental awareness, meeting the needs of the child is synonymous with meeting the needs of the parent. For these parents, reasoning methods are chosen because they are successful in changing behavior the parents find undesirable; the criterion for success is suppression of the behavior, not change in the motives of the child. The answers to the following questions exemplify the egoistic level.

> **What do you rely on most to get your children to mind you?**
> I threaten the children with a spoon. I have one of those spoons with the little holes, to strain peas and things, so I take that, and say, "If you don't be good, I am going to beat you with it." They usually behave when they see it. I do not use it, but when they see it, they usually behave.
> **How does that seem to work?**
> They do mind, up to a certain point, and then they say, "Mommy is not going to spank me," so I will start all over again.
> **Why do you use that method?**
> It seems to be about the only method that works.
> **Do you think it is the best way?**
> Well, no, but I do not know of any other way that works as well.

Level 2—Conventional. At this level, the needs of the child can be discriminated from those of the parent, but only in terms of children's universal requirements rather than the particular needs of an individual child. The reasons given for discipline and authority are not simply to change behavior but to instill standards and values that will guide the child's actions in the future. Thus, the child's understanding of the reasons for punishment is considered central. The parent explains why what the child is doing is wrong to ensure the inclusion of his or her standards into the child's developing value system. For example:

> **What do you rely on most to get your children to do what you want them to and not what you don't want them to?**
> We explain everything. We explain what is good and what is not good, and explain why. Thus, he can make a

decision as to whether he is going to go along with it or not. Then we try to reinforce our ideas.
Why is explaining important?
So the child will know himself what is right and wrong.

When describing how needs are met, the focus of reasoning at this level shifts from what the parent does to how it affects children emotionally:

What do you feel children need most from their parents?
Love (explain). It is important just to let them know that you love them, that you care, and that you are concerned about what they do. Just try to be the best parent you can.
Why do you think that is most important, conveying that love?
Because if children know they have love, then they are secure.

Level 3—Individualistic. At the individualistic level, parents understand that the child is an unique individual who is known through the parent-child relationship rather than by external definitions of children. Parental reasoning differentiates this child from children in general, so that the needs of the child as an individual are considered. The parent reasons that behavior has a cause and that to change behavior, its cause, rather than its impact, must be addressed. Thus, the why of the child's thinking and behavior is considered in addition to the behavior itself.

What do you feel children need most from their parents?
Love and time. They also need to have their needs considered. They are not always happy with the things that we do and with the things that we want to make them happy. You must look at *them,* and if they do not tell you, you must ask them. You have to try to find out what they want and what is going on in their heads.
Let us get back to the subject of discipline. What do you feel is the best way to get a child to mind you?
Talking.
Why is that the best way?
Because first of all, you ask questions, and then you find

out why they did it, and they tell you, "I broke it because you were not paying any attention to me." So you find out, "What did you want me to do?" Then I explain that I was busy too but after I finish, I will have time to talk or play a game.

Level 4—Analytic. At this highest level of parental reasoning, the child is seen as a complex and ever-changing psychological self-system that interacts with the parents' systems. Thus, the child and the parents are perceived as autonomous as well as interdependent. Needs are defined as more than specific requirements of the child; needs are processes considered within a framework of change, adjustment, and growth.

What do you feel children need most from their parents?
I think they need their time. In terms of how to deal with the world, they need to know how the parents deal with the world, because that is how they are going to learn how to deal with it.
Why do you feel that is so important?
Because I think it is the only thing they do not pick up on their own. When children first start having a social life at two or three years old, they do not have the emotional capability of dealing with relationships and coming out on top. I think they need to draw that from their parents' training in order to learn to deal with other children, to deal with their feelings about the world, and to cope with the outside world.

In this example, the need to learn how to cope with the world is a continuing process of interaction and integration between the child's evolving sense of the self and the child's experience of others. How one understands and deals with one's feelings and oneself is connected with how one copes with the world.

Newberger's analysis of levels of parental awareness is not only a method for clarifying the distinctiveness of each parent's way of making sense of child-rearing, but also a means of uncovering a potential source of parental dysfunction. Newberger's research indicates that there is a relationship between the way parents think and the way they behave toward their children.

The Relationship of Parental Awareness to Parental Functioning

It seems that parents who reason at a very low level of parental awareness are more likely to be inadequate in their parental roles. But perhaps with strong supports in their lives, such parents would be able to raise their children appropriately. Conversely, it seems that parents who reason at a very high level of awareness are the most likely to raise their children well. But, under extreme stress, even these parents might have serious difficulties. The potential relationships between parental awareness level, the stresses and strengths in the family environment, and the probability of parental dysfunction are illustrated in Table 4.

Table 4. Parental Awareness Level and Parent-Child Relationship

	Average Level of Reasoning	
	Low Parental Awareness	*High Parental Awareness*
Stress environment	High probability of dysfunction	Possible dysfunction
Average expectable support	Possible dysfunction	Low probability of dysfunction

Note.—Reprinted with permission from Newberger CM: The cognitive structure of parenthood: designing a descriptive measure. In *New Directions for Child Development,* vol. 7. Edited by Selman R, Yando R. San Francisco, Jossey-Bass, 1980, pp 45–67.

An urban sample of eight parents with histories of having abused or neglected a child was matched with a control group on social class, race, and ages and number of children. The data on levels of parental awareness was correlated to the level of parental functioning as indicated in clinical records and case histories. It was found that the egoistic level 1 awareness was the most prevalent type of understanding in the neglect/abuse group, and that the mean level of parental awareness was significantly lower for the neglect/abuse group than for the control group.

These findings point to a need for interventions on parental reasoning, perhaps in the form of education. Newberger suggests two intervention modalities—family intervention and parent group intervention. Family intervention would provide interpersonal experiences with family members, such as mutual problem-solving or discussions of feelings and perspectives about family problems and family issues. In parental awareness groups, the traditional emphasis on group support and child development information may be supplemented with the presentation of hypothetical or actual parent-child conflict dilemmas to be dilemmas to be discussed by the group. This addition might aid parents in considering what they would do in a variety of problem-solving situations involving their children and child-rearing decisions.

INTERACTION OF MULTIPLE FACTORS CONTRIBUTING TO HIGH-RISK PARENTING

Henry N. Ricciuti, Ph.D.[1]

Introduction

Ricciuti presents a review of the evidence relevant to the interactions among factors contributing to the increased probability of high-risk parenting, particularly in the first three years of life. Because single-factor explanations are inadequate, Ricciuti developed an interactional multifactor high-risk parenting model containing key variables derived from the research review. Ricciuti summarizes and illustrates a variety of factors associated with high-risk parenting and adverse developmental outcomes. These antecedent factors may be

---

[1] This paper was prepared by Dr. Ricciuti in collaboration with Rebekah Dorman, B.A.

found in characteristics of the mother (e.g., age or health status) or of the child (e.g., low birth weight or developmental anomalies), in the family setting and available supports, and in the larger social environment and circumstances under which families live (e.g., housing, jobs, health care, or support services). Two of these risk factors discussed in some detail are adolescent childbearing and the effects of bearing a premature or low birth weight baby. Three illustrative negative outcomes considered in relation to multiple-antecedent risk factors are child abuse, neglect, and failure to thrive.

In examining these factors, investigators have tended to treat them singly or independently rather than as a complex interdependent system of antecedents that change over time. Although the effects of biology and the environment are considered primary, the individual's experiences over time and personal perceptions of events have not been adequately studied.

Potential threats to normal parenting represent not only challenging theoretical issues but also the practical challenge of defining and implementing useful strategies for prevention and intervention. Identifying appropriate strategies requires that parenting and the factors impinging on it be conceptualized as an interactional network; otherwise, solutions will be too simplistic to be effective.

Ricciuti notes that it is important to direct equal attention to the ways in which particular factors interact to decrease the risks to parenting and child development. In analyzing the role of multiple factors in high-risk parenting, one must understand not only how they combine to exacerbate risk but also how they might interact to enhance parenting and development. Information from this standpoint is critical for guiding interventions because it allows for positive goals and for building strengths.

Similarly, Ricciuti believes that our understanding of high-risk parenting would be clarified if we learned why some parents and children who are considered at risk in fact fail to show the adverse developmental outcomes expected on the basis of the indicators. The examination of "counter-risk" or protective factors that contribute to the coping strengths of children and families also aid in the development of prevention and intervention measures.

Interactions among Multiple-Risk Factors

In Ricciuti's view, all outcomes must be considered in terms of multiple, interacting antecedents. As examples, he cites child abuse, neglect, and failure to thrive.

Child Abuse and Neglect. Until recently, the literature on the antecedent conditions of child abuse and neglect has focused on single-factor causal explanations. Risk factors studied in this manner include: stress, social isolation, parents' personality temperamentally difficult children, parental attitudes, neonatal separation, parents' age, bonding failure, parents' child-rearing history, economic conditions, and the cultural milieu.

Ricciuti notes that while it is clearly absurd to suggest that all parents who experience stress, have a difficult child, or are young, are likely to abuse their children, this is the implication of single-factor theories. In addition, the retrospective design of most studies on child abuse and neglect has served to limit research, since this approach necessarily ignores those parents with the same elements of risk who do not mistreat their children.

Recent prospective studies have uncovered multiple-risk factors linked to child abuse and neglect. In one study, mistreating parents of premature or ill infants were more likely to be judged as impulsive/apathetic, futile, childish/dependent, and illiterate. At the same time, these mothers were coping with more extreme social stress conditions and had infants who were small, premature, and had more congenital defects. Although more risk factors are now being identified and considered in combination, the studies do not yet present a consistent picture of the definitive factors or combinations.

Failure to Thrive. Failure to thrive is severe growth failure in the first few years of life that is not explainable in terms of organic disease or the availability of food. This is a very puzzling condition, the etiology of which is not fully understood, although it occurs most commonly in families characterized by a high degree of stress and disruption. Like child abuse and neglect, failure to thrive is an early developmental disturbance that can be understood only in the context of interactions among multiple-risk factors. The search for antecedent factors has probed unfavorable characteristics of the mother and her background, as well as the contemporary social, economic, or environmental stresses confronting her and the family. More recently, attention has also been directed at the role played by infant characteristics, which may pose special demands on the mother, significantly affecting the patterns of mother-infant interaction in the early months of life. Research findings suggest that all of these factors contribute to the failure-to-thrive condition. However, no one factor appears to be overriding, and it appears that the threat to the child is increased with the increase of risk factors.

Multiple-Risk Factor Model

Ricciuti developed a multiple-risk factor model (Figure 2), based on the hypothesis that common threads or sets of factors are shared as antecedents to a number of adverse parenting and developmental outcomes or that might operate protectively to reduce such outcomes, despite acknowledged risk conditions.

The quality of early child care and rearing provided by the parents can be affected favorably or unfavorably by positive or negative features of the molar or broad social environment in which the family lives, by features of the family environment, by the mother's or primary caregiver's own characteristics, and by the individual characteristics of the child.

In addition, there are important linkages between these antecedent-risk or counter-risk factors and their impact on parenting behavior. For example, potential adverse outcomes of a particular risk condition, such as very young maternal age, may be exacerbated cumulatively when combined with other high-risk conditions (e.g., poverty, isolation, poor prenatal care, or a premature or "difficult" infant). In the real world, these factors tend to be naturally linked,

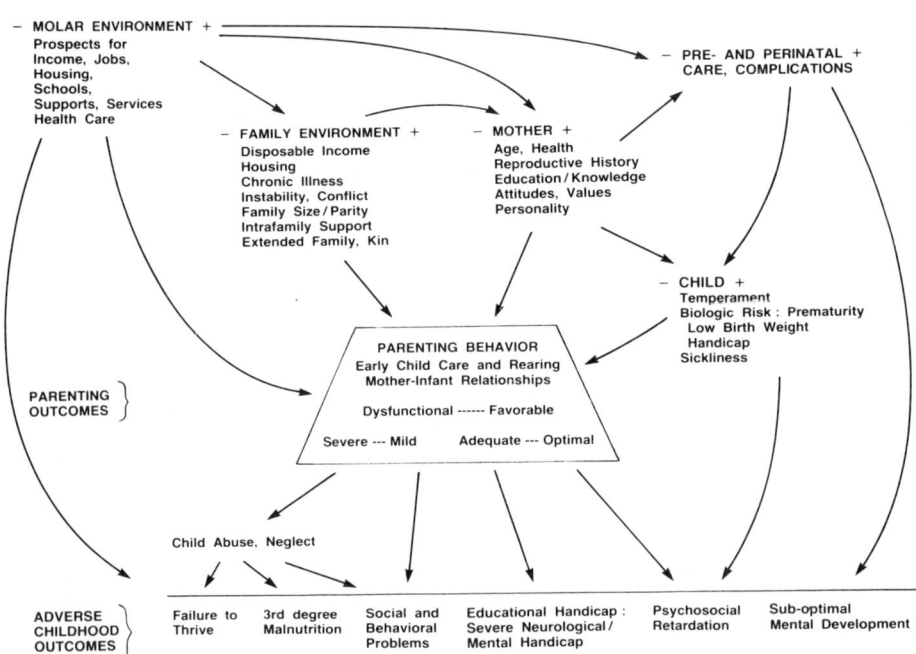

Figure 2. Multiple-risk factor model.

adding to the risk. At the same time, however, positive or protective factors may help counteract the adverse impact of particular risk factors.

Ricciuti concludes that the primary goal of preventive intervention should be the enhancement of the family's and primary caregiver's ability to provide a growth-promoting child-care environment. As a more complete understanding of the interactions among various risk factors is achieved, better guidelines for the planning of sensitive and effective intervention strategies can be developed.

PARENTING IN INFANCY AND EARLY CHILDHOOD: A DEVELOPMENTAL STRUCTURALIST APPROACH TO DELINEATING ADAPTIVE AND MALADAPTIVE PATTERNS

Stanley I. Greenspan, M.D.

Introduction

Greenspan's research, which has led to the formulation of a developmental structuralist approach to assessment and intervention, examines the demand characteristics of each subphase of infancy and early childhood. The infant and mother or other caregivers are viewed as separate units within a system requiring a high level of integration to function optimally. High risk exists when mother-infant integration is poor in terms of stage-specific needs or demands. Intervention, even at later stages, led to improved functioning.

An essential component of parenting is the facilitation of the child's progress at each specific stage of development. Greenspan delineates the key stage-specific tasks for each phase of development during infancy and early childhood, using his developmental structuralist approach, which allows for the study of the interaction of consitutional, maturational, environmental, and parenting patterns. According to this approach, the successful resolution of each developmental phase requires that the environment, particularly the parents, provide the appropriate patterns of care, or experiential ingredients, to foster growth. It is important to note that each phase of development demands a different environmental response, making flexibility and adaptability important parental characteristics. The degree of parental risk depends, in part, on the inability or unwillingness to adjust to the developmental requirements of the child.

In the developmental structuralist view, the child and each parent are considered self-consistent units interacting within the family system. The child organizes his or her experiences at each developmental stage according to the characteristics of that stage and the quality of the environment. Emotional and cognitive growth are continuous processes that depend on the functioning of each unit in the system, and the system as a synergystic entity greater than the sum of its parts.

Stages of Development

The stages of cognitive-socioemotional development are described in Table 5, which includes illustrations of adaptive and maladaptive capacities and environments at each stage.

Assessment of Development in Infancy

One of the infant's first tasks is to adapt to the external environment while maintaining a state of internal regulation, including basic neurophysiological processes and the rhythms of sleep-wake and hunger cycles. This capacity is viewed as a stage-specific structural tendency to strive for homeostasis. Some infants, according to individual constitutional differences and environmental influences, can remain alert and engage the world in a multisensory affective manner in the context of internal regulation and regular cyclic patterns. They are able to console themselves or are easily consoled. Other infants, left to their own devices, are unable to regulate their internal processes, becoming hyperexcitable and irritable, with varying degrees of engagement with the external world, depending on the capacity of their caregivers to help them achieve equilibrium.

At the next stage, between ages two and four months, infants begin to demonstrate a unique investment in people and capacity for forming human attachments. This is one of their first and most important developmental tasks. A special interest evolves in those caregivers who are relatively permanent in their environment; this is evidenced by the social smile. In addition, infants at this stage show individual differences in communication patterns and affect expressed and experienced in their special dyadic attachments. In assessing an infant's response to this fundamental step, the answers to the following questions should be considered:

> Is this a warm, loving dyad where infant and mother both experience a range of affects from deep, rich pleasure to assertiveness and protest, or is it a shallow, mechanical attachment, devoid of affect, behavioral richness, and flexibility?
>
> What are the sensory modalities used by the infant and the mother? Are they visually, audibly, vocally, and tactilely connected, or are only one or two of these modalities used?
>
> What is the range of motor involvement?
>
> Do these experiential organizations exist only intermittently, or are they the usual mode of involvement?
>
> Can the dyad re-engage after a disruption?
>
> Are unique personal characteristics beginning to express themselves?
>
> Do special games or preferred affects and sensorimotor patterns characterize this relationship?

If an affective and relatively pleasurable attachment is formed (an investment in the human, animate world), then with maturation the infant develops complex patterns of communication within this primary human relationship. Parallel with the infant's relationship to the inanimate world, where basic schemes of causality are being developed (means-ends relationships), the infant becomes capable of complicated human communications.

Evidence that means-ends relationships are established between the

Table 5. Stages of Development

Stage	Age	Adaptive Abilities
Homeostasis	0 to 3 months	Internal regulation (harmony) and balanced interest in the world
Attachment	2 to 7 months	Rich, deep, multisensory emotional investment in animate world (especially with primary caregivers)
Somatopsychological differentiation	3 to 10 months	Flexible, wide-ranging affective multisystem contingent (reciprocal) interactions (especially with primary caregivers)
Behavioral organization, initiative, and internalization	9 to 24 months	Complex, organized, assertive, innovative, and integrated behavioral and emotional patterns
Representational capacity: differentiation and consolidation	Representational capacity: 1½ to 2½ years Differentiation and consolidation: 2½ to 4 years	Formation and elaboration of internal representations (imagery; organization and differentiation of imagery pertaining to self and others; emergence of cognitive insight; stabilization of mood; gradual emergence of basic personality functions such as reality testing, and impulse regulation)
Capacity of limited extended representational systems and multiple extended representational systems	Middle childhood through adolescence	Enhanced and eventually optimal flexibility to conserve and transform complex and organized representations of experience in the context of expanded relationship patterns

Maladaptive Abilities	Adaptive Environment	Maladaptive Environment
Unregulated (e.g., hyperexcitable), withdrawn (apathetic)	Invested, dedicated, protective, comforting, predictable, engaging, and interesting	Unavailable, chaotic, dangerous, abusive, hypo- or hyper-stimulating, and dull
Total lack of, or non-effective, shallow, impersonal, involvement (e.g., autistic patterns) in animate world	In love and woos infant to "fall in love" with emotional, multi-sensory pleasurable involvement	Emotionally distant, aloof, and impersonal (highly ambivalent)
Behavior and affect random or chaotic, narrow, rigid, and stereotyped	Reads and responds contingently to infant's communications across multiple sensory and affective systems	Ignores or misreads (e.g., projection) infant's communications (e.g., the overly intrusive, preoccupied, or depressed caregiver)
Fragmented, stereotyped, and polarized behavior and emotions (e.g., withdrawn, compliant, hyperaggressive, or disorganized toddler)	Admiring of toddler's initiative and autonomy, yet available, tolerant and firm; follows toddler's lead and helps him organize diverse behavioral and affective elements	Overly intrusive, controlling; fragmented, fearful (especially of toddler's autonomy); abruptly and prematurely separates
No representational (symbolic) elaboration; behavior and affect concrete, shallow, polarized; sense of self and other fragmented, undifferentiated, narrow, and rigid; impaired reality testing, impulse regulation, and mood stabilization	Emotionally available to phase-appropriate regressions and dependency needs; reads, responds to, and encourages symbolic elaboration across behavioral and emotional domains while fostering reality orientation and internalization of limits	Fearful of, or denies phase-appropriate needs; engages child only in concrete (nonsymbolic) modes generally or in certain realms (e.g., around pleasure), or misreads or responds noncontingently or nonrealistically to emerging communications; overly permissive or punitive
Derivative representational capacities limited or defective, as are latency and adolescent relationships and coping abilities	Supports more complex phase- and age-appropriate experiential and interpersonal development	Conflicted over child's age-appropriate propensities (e.g., competitiveness, pleasure orientation, growing competence, assertiveness, and self-sufficiency; becomes aloof or maintains symbolic tie; and withdraws from or overly engages in competitive or pleasurable strivings

infant and the primary caregiver is the infant's growing ability to distinguish the caregiver from others and to differentiate his own actions from the consequences of these actions affectively, somatically, behaviorally, and interpersonally. Differentiation begins to occur along a number of developmental lines, such as sensorimotor integration, affects, and relationships. A third developmental stage therefore centers on differentiation and may be called somatopsychological differentiation to indicate processes occurring at the somatic (e.g., sensorimotor) and emerging psychological levels. Although schemes of causality are being established in relation to the interpersonal world, it is not at all clear that these schemes exist at an organized representational or symbolic level. Rather, they appear to exist for the most part at a somatic level, some perhaps even prenatally determined, even though we do observe the precursors of representational capacities.

With appropriate reading of cues and systematic differential responses, the behavioral repertoire of the infant or toddler becomes more complicated, and communications take on more organized, meaningful configurations. By 12 months the infant is able to begin connecting behavioral units to form larger organizations; for example, complex emotional responses such as affiliation, wariness, and fear. Further into the second year of life, in the practicing subphase of the development of individuation, the capacity evolves for forming original behavioral schemes and increased imitative activity and intentionality.

A type of learning through imitation, evidenced in earlier development, now seems to take a more dominant role. As imitations develop a more integrated, personal form, it appears the toddler is "taking on" or internalizing attributes of his caretakers. To describe these new capacities it is useful to consider a fourth stage, centering on complex organized emotional and behavioral patterns, that is, behavioral organization, initiative, and internalization.

Toward the end of the second year, when the toddler's central nervous system matures further, increased ability to form and organize mental representations appears, and an additional set of steps can be described.

When assessing along the continuum from adaptability to pathology, Greenspan suggests the inclusion of the following parameters: range and depth of age and phase-appropriate experience; stability of experiential organization, including integrative capacity and resilience to stress; and individual personal characteristics. The better the adaptation at earlier stages, the better the chance for adaptation at later stages. For example, an infant who begins warding off affectionate, intimate behavior is unlikely, unless the trend is reversed, to learn the skills of intimacy. On the other hand, the infant who organizes experiences of physical closeness and interpersonal affection is more likely to have an opportunity to learn the later forms of intimate behavior.

Assessing psychopathological as well as adaptive patterns in infants, toddlers, and their families becomes especially important in light of the fact that the most serious maladaptive patterns, including severe problems in homeostasis, attachment, and somatopsychological differentiation most likely occur with great frequency. Estimates of the challenge of the multiple-risk-factor families to health and mental health services indicate a major public problem. It is estimated that such families constitute the 6 percent of the population that use over 50 percent of all public health, mental health, and social services. Without intervention, these families often deteriorate further in their survival ability with each subsequent child. With intervention, most families are able to reverse this pattern of functional deterioration, and their new children are helped to function competently.

Intervention with Families at Risk

Greenspan has used the developmental structuralist approach as the foundation of his longitudinal research on parent-child interaction, which is directed toward the goal of designing and implementing effective intervention strategies in families considered to be maladapted. In this study, participants are involved prenatally and followed for five years or more postnatally with a focus on assessing multiple lines of development, including physical and neurological cognitive and socioemotional, in the context of family and community. Preventive and treatment services, offered as clinically appropriate, are tailored to the individual requirements of each infant, young child, and family. Unique to this program has been the ability to work with the most challenging multiple-risk-factor families, who do not usually avail themselves of traditional health and mental health services. These families often contain within one unit such risk factors as mental illness, violence, history of child abuse and neglect, low educational status, and poor prenatal care. They may also be associated with high rates of infant morbidity and mortality.

On a case-by-case basis, preventive intervention was successful in a very high percentage of the cases in this study. The earlier the intervention, the more rapid the recovery to an optimal pattern of development. Even in cases of severe depression, psychotic and borderline conditions in the parents, and unpropitious constitutional patterns in the infant, interventions using the developmental structuralist model led to improvement and age-appropriate behavior in children. This suggests that the impact of maladaptive early experiences can be reversed to some extent, depending on many factors, including the age of the child at intervention, the staffing capacity for simultaneous work with the infant and his or her family in a combined outreach and center-based program, and the staff's technical expertise in pinpointing precise factors in the infant, family, and community structure that undermine the achievement of adaptive phase-specific development.

SUMMARY COMMENTS

Stanley I. Greenspan, M.D.

The real challenge in understanding high-risk parenting seems to be the search for an appropriate construct, the grouping of the set of functions that we mean when we refer to "high risk." This meeting has provided an outstanding representation of all the levels of inquiry needed to cope with this complex issue. We have macroscopic approaches based on large data pools such as socioeconomic class, and we have microscopic examinations such as specific mother behavior, with the clinical descriptive level falling somewhere in between.

Howard Osofsky led off the discussion of high-risk parenting as opposed to normal parenting. He introduced us to the complexity of the issue, reminding us that such concerns as parent-child bonding are not sufficient alone and that it is perilously easy to isolate yourself and concentrate on a limited focus.

Elizabeth McAnarney presented some of the macroscopic data in terms of the sociological literature on adolescent parenting, the attempt to evaluate the explanatory factors, and the debate over the age factor in the adolescent mother. I think the question remains, but clearly the combination of extreme youth with poor prenatal care and concomitant factors offers some explanatory value. However, she also attempts to answer the more difficult question of how these factors affect the transmission of care from family to infant and infant to family. Here she is struggling with the microscopic issues, such as "picking, poking, and pinching," and the challenge is much the same. At what level of abstraction do we try to look at some of these factors; do we group "picking, poking, and pinching" with four or five other behaviors and come up with a construct that will have more explanatory value than any one alone?

Vivian Shapiro then broadened our perspective from the clinical viewpoint, sharing with us the conclusions she and Selma Frieberg and their colleagues at Michigan have developed over the years and also the challenge of trying to take clinical case material and organize it into conceptually meaningful categories. My own bias is that the clinical situation provides an intermediate conceptual level between the macroscopic and the microscopic.

So, having gone from the macroscopic to the clinical level, we proceed to the microscopic with the challenges presented by Carol Aradine, who focused on the specific issue of parents of chronically ill children and the special problems they face, such as divided family time and the need for constant vigilance. Here the researchers' problems include the impossibility of predicting which families will do well in this situation and the relative lack of study in this area of high-risk parenting. Few organized research attempts focus on this, and the field is a complicated one as the issues change at each developmental phase, not only for the ill child in the family but for subsequent and older children. Each child presents a new developmental challenge to a family that is affected by a major event—the illness itself. These complicated dynamics present a most provocative question.

Sherry Johnson-Soderberg focused our attention on specific issues of mourning. Here again the issue is a complicated one because the mourning process, or the broader process of loss, creates the special issue of replacement children and the subsequent impact on them. Where parental mourning remains unresolved, the door is opened to a whole series of potential studies.

Suzanne Hall Johnson again brought us down to a specific area: premature infants, their separation from the parents, and the stresses inherent in this situation. (This raises more generic questions, such as how to deal with this devastating situation, centered around the low birth weight and the infant's struggle to survive, where each infant is unique.) Complex staff-infant and staff-parent interactions enter the picture. Not only the perinatal phases but subsequent developmental phases present important issues, and we are still working toward the right constructs for dealing with them.

Eli and Carolyn Newberger broadened our perspective by looking at a specific problem of child abuse and neglect and reflecting that this is part of a generic category of maladaptive parenting. In looking at Eli's paper, I see the similarities between failure-to-thrive infants, abused children, and other situations. Eli suggests the existence of a common syndrome. We have not yet elicited the specific factors pointing to the infant who will be physically hurt and abused, who will be neglected, who will fail to thrive, or who will develop other problems not yet even identified in infants, such as signaling problems. I think Carolyn points to the same issue by considering the parents' social cognition and sense of perspective.

Henry Ricciuti has summarized for us the many factors that influence good and poor outcomes in child-rearing. He also provides us with a concept on the causality of high-risk parenting that goes beyond biological and environmental effects to a transactional model that considers these factors with the child's and parents' reactions to them and to each other over time.

How do we move from these constructs, these excellent first steps in considering the vulnerability or inflexibility in the family system or the individual parent? How do we progress to the specific level, so that we can improve our clinical prognoses?

I think the challenge is similar to that of the early work with schizophrenic families. When we are talking about problems and parenting, we begin to see common features that overlap. And that, at least, is a starting point.

PART III
PREVENTION OF HIGH-RISK PARENTING OUTCOMES

The presentations and comments comprising Part III address the issues surrounding the prevention of high-risk parenting outcomes. Some of the questions raised include: Who should be the target of intervention? What types of programs and strategies are most effective and for whom? How can we increase the communication between parents and health providers? Are prevention and intervention efforts cost-effective?

Olds, Hoover, and Hoekelman agree that prevention programs should be made available to all first-time parents rather than being limited to only those families identified as high risk. New parenthood is a difficult and stressful transition regardless of specific, identifiable risk factors. All expectant and new parents can benefit from specialized help during both the prenatal and perinatal phases. These investigators also agree that more research focused directly on prevention/intervention strategies is needed to determine their effectiveness.

Robert A. Hoekelman, M.D.

AN INTERVENTION PROGRAM FOR HIGH-RISK FAMILIES

David L. Olds, Ph.D.

Introduction

Olds describes a multifaceted prevention/intervention nurse home visitation program for high-risk families. Although available to all first-time parents in the target community, active recruitment focused on families in which first-time parents were teenagers, unmarried, or poor. Nurses engaged in three basic activities: providing parents with information on fetal and infant development, involving significant family members and friends as supports, and linking the families to relevant community services. Potential side effects are considered, and program evaluation efforts are discussed.

A nurse home-visitation program, known as the Prenatal/Early Infancy Project, was carried out in a semirural county in the Appalachian region of New York. Services were made available to anyone in the community bearing a first infant, but the program focused on families possessing certain risk characteristics, specifically, being an adolescent, unmarried, or of low socioeconomic status. These parents are considered at high risk because of the higher levels of stress with which they must contend, often resulting in childhood disorders, including premature birth, low birth weight, growth and nutritional problems, accidents, various childhood illnesses, developmental delays, behavior problems, and child maltreatment. The overriding concern of the program was to promote the health and development of children in the context of the family and the community.

Initiating the program during pregnancy was considered critical for successful outcome. Home visitation began before the twenty-fourth week of pregnancy, with visits being made about twice a month and continuing through the second year of the infants' lives, with less frequent visits as they grew older. Intervention during pregnancy was considered important in terms of: developing an effective, caring relationship with parents; encouraging the acceptance of support during the biological, psychological, and social crises of this period; supplying useful information and emotional support; and preventing low birth weight and prematurity.

Parents were considered the most important environmental influences on the health and development of children. Parent behavior and the parent-child relationship were viewed and treated as embedded in systems of informal social networks and formal relationships with health and human service providers, both of which could play powerful roles in supporting or undermining the interactions between parents and their children. The program provided for addressing specific parental behaviors that theoretically affect fetal and infant health. It was designed to be fairly short-term, efficient, thorough, and acceptable to both the families and the representatives of a wide political spectrum.

In terms of specific services, the nurses engaged in three basic activities designed to improve conditions for pregnancy, birth, and early child-rearing. These activities included: (1) providing parents with a home-based education program that focused on factors influencing fetal and infant development, thereby promoting positive health and caregiving behaviors; (2) involving, in a systematic way, significant relatives and friends whom mothers wanted to participate in the home visits, in an attempt to create a more supportive, informal environment for bearing and rearing children; and (3) linking families with other health and human services in the community so that the families' basic health and survival needs could be met.

These activities were conceptualized by Olds as interrelated in the model represented in Figure 1, with the growing fetus and child considered the central focus. The parents are viewed as having the most direct impact on the health and development of the fetus and child. Health and human services and friends and relatives are each viewed as having a potential impact on parental attitudes and behavior toward the child. This outer ring can be either supportive or stressful. One purpose of this intervention program was to minimize the stress and maximize the support value of this outer ring to give the most benefit to parent and child.

Parent Education

Parent education was the first major nurse activity. A basic premise of the program was that a sense of caring and a strong alliance between nurses and parents were necessary ingredients for

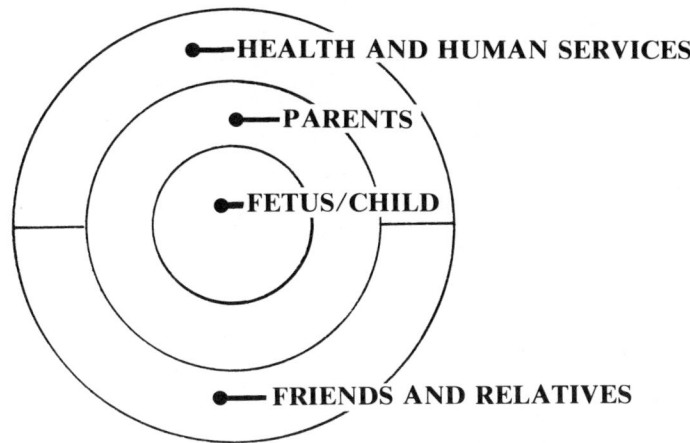

Figure 1. Intervention model for high-risk families.

successful outcome. In the context of trust and respect, parents would be more likely to accept the advice and support of home visitors. The nurses tried to establish this emotional tone by listening to parents' concerns, showing respect for family members, and sharing some of their own experiences as parents. As part of this educational process, the home visitors strove to strengthen the mothers' feelings of adequacy and self-confidence, give them more control, and reduce their guilt.

Assessment was an important component of the education process. The nurses listened to the parents tell about their own child-rearing histories and their knowledge, attitudes, and beliefs about pregnancy and early child-rearing. Evaluation of risk also involved gathering information concerning current stresses, parental expectations, and emotional problems in the family. Emotional problems, such as poor impulse control and mood lability, could have a negative impact in early infancy, particularly under adverse circumstances, such as being a single parent or bearing an infant who is passive or difficult temperamentally. A sound assessment of such factors allowed the home visitors to be more responsive to the families' needs.

The specific content of the educational program was based on what is currently known in the field. During the first and second trimesters of pregnancy, a major portion of the prenatal program focused on helping women to improve their diets and cut down or eliminate smoking, drinking, and drugs. Nurses provided information on the physiology of pregnancy, fetal development, stages of labor and delivery, and how each of these processes can be affected by maternal health habits. It was felt that this information would motivate mothers to improve their health habits. In cases in which mothers were unwilling or unable to change, information was communicated in such a way as to minimize guilt and anxiety.

The next phases started about the twenty-eighth week of pregnancy when the parents' attention turned toward labor, delivery, and the early care of the infant. At this point, the nurses helped prepare mothers for these experiences in both practical and emotional ways. The basic approach was to provide guidance and support to allow parents to rehearse and plan appropriately.

The enhancement of parental adaptation continued after the infant was born. The nurses visited mothers and babies in the hospital and again in the home about three days after they were discharged. In the hospital, the nurses were present for the discharge examination so that they could hear the physician's specific instructions and reinforce his advice later on.

While emphasis was placed on the needs and characteristics of the infants, the mothers' needs were addressed as well. The nurses were continually aware of the extent to which the mothers were coping with early child care and adjusting to the postpartum period. Some of the topics covered at this time included the resumption of sexual relations, birth control, schooling, and employment.

During the first few months of the new infant's life, parents received help with physical care and feeding, information on newborn behavior, advice on home and car safety, and counseling, support, and, where necessary, referral for additional help. As the infant progressed through the first year, education was provided on what to expect and how to cope with the changes in a variety of areas, from toilet training to baby proofing the house.

A special attempt was made to avoid pressuring the parents or seeming to interfere. These potential problems were anticipated and discussed openly with the parents, thereby increasing the alliance with them.

Involving Relatives and Friends

Part of the outer ring in Figure 1 included friends and relatives. The role of these support people was reinforced as much as possible, as long as they remained supportive in the eyes of the parents.

Mothers were asked to identify one person living outside their home to whom they could turn at any time, day or night, if they needed help. This type of support can be invaluable under stressful circumstances. Without any support of this kind, the early care of the newborn can be overwhelming. This would be particularly true when the father was absent. About 60 percent of the women in the program were unmarried when they enrolled, and about 10 percent of these were living alone.

To facilitate the involvement of other family members and friends, the nurses paid special attention to their needs and interests and helped them participate in the home visits. This inclusion of other supportive individuals promoted the expression of values and beliefs from the family and from the parents' subculture, minimizing the potential for nurse interference. In addition, this involvement diminished parental dependency on the nurses.

Linkages with Formal Services

The second half of the outer ring in Figure 1 includes health and human services. Consistent attempts were made to keep the lines of communication open between the parents and relevant community services. Parents were routinely encouraged to keep prenatal appointments and to enroll in childbirth education classes. The nurses sent regular reports to the primary care providers, and contacted them by phone when necessary to discuss special problems. For the significant number of families in the program who lived in isolated rural regions, transportation was provided for prenatal and well-child care at the physicans' offices.

Although practical and emotional support was offered to facilitate the parents' trust and use of these services, the ultimate goal was to foster their independence of action. This balance was a goal throughout the phases of the program.

Some of the problems met by these and other interventions included: home visit appointments that were chronically cancelled, forgotten, or ignored; initial skepticism or resistance to outsiders; parental apathy about the material presented; networks of friends and relatives that created more stress for parents than support; the absence of systematic social and economic supports for meeting families' basic needs for survival; and parental resistance to participation in social programs. These obstacles were dealt with as they arose on a step-by-step problem-solving basis.

Program Evaluation

Was parent support effective? The program is presently being analyzed to determine whether specific components were especially influential, whether observed improvements in child health could be attributed to certain processes set in motion by the program, and whether certain families benefited more than others.

In order to evaluate effectiveness, 401 families (85 percent of whom were at risk) were randomly assigned into four distinct service conditions, three of which represented subsets of total intervention described. All four groups received early and periodic health screening; the second, third, and fourth groups received free transportation for regular prenatal and well-child care throughout pregnancy and the first two years postpartum; the third and fourth groups received nurse home-visitation during pregnancy; the fourth groups also received visitation during the first two years of the child's life. By comparing the mothers and children receiving these different services, Olds and his colleagues will be able to determine the effectiveness of different components of the overall intervention.

Outcome variables consisted of critical aspects of the child's health and development. It was hypothesized that the program would be effective to the extent that it positively affected maternal health habits, the support of friends and relatives, and parents' use of community services. It was further hypothesized that parents at moderate risk would benefit the most, while those at either extreme risk or minimal risk would benefit least. Data analyses are currently being carried out to test these hypotheses.

In terms of Old's research, firm conclusions cannot be drawn because the research is not yet completed. Preliminary results from the pregnancy phase of the project, however, have shown that those women followed by a nurse understood and made better use of community services, had husbands or boyfriends who showed a greater interest in their pregnancy, were more frequently accompanied by someone into the labor room, and reduced their smoking more by the end of pregnancy than women in the control groups. Future analyses will focus on understanding the implications of these behavioral and family system changes for improved fetal growth and parents' later capacity to care for their newborn.

PERINATAL COACHING: A PRIMARY PREVENTION MODEL

Leslie Hoover, R.N., M.A.

Introduction

Hoover describes a perinatal coaching model aimed at the prevention of child abuse and neglect and based on the premise that all first-time parents can benefit from supportive services. Because parenthood is a critical transitional period for all new parents, Hoover believes that prevention/intervention programs should not be directed only to high-risk families. All new parents can benefit from acquiring specific skills to increase their confidence, competence, and satisfaction in their new role.

A second premise underlying the perinatal coaching model is that enhanced interactions between parents and infants early in life promote a positive bond between parent and child and have a positive impact on future interactions. When early parent-infant contacts are supplemented with information about normal infant behaviors and practice in interpreting and responding to infant messages, the parents gain new confidence in their own abilities and learn that their new infant is a unique individual, capable of communicating with them on a nonverbal level. When parents are given permission, encouragement, and training in responding to the infant, attachment is promoted.

The third and final premise of the perinatal coaching model is that the teaching of interpersonal and interactional skills is the element missing from our present health services delivery system. Prenatal and postpartum contacts with health-care professionals emphasize cognitive learning about pregnancy, the labor and delivery processes, and physical care of the newborn. However, time is rarely set aside to discuss the infant's social capabilities and to practice interacting with the child. In a perinatal coaching program, the coach not only provides information but also teaches actual psychomotor skills, offers opportunities for practice, and provides rapid, constructive feedback on parental behavior. These behaviors are broken down into component parts for ease of learning, presented in a step-by-step sequence, and demonstrated by the coach.

Infants communicate using their sensory systems and rely heavily on nonverbal behavior. Appropriate parent-child interactions at this stage require adaptation on the parents' part to these unfamiliar types of communication and stimuli. The infant must be capable of sending clear cues to the parent, who must be able to receive, interpret, and respond to these cues. The parent-infant interaction process is conceptualized in the Barnard Model, as shown in Figure 2.

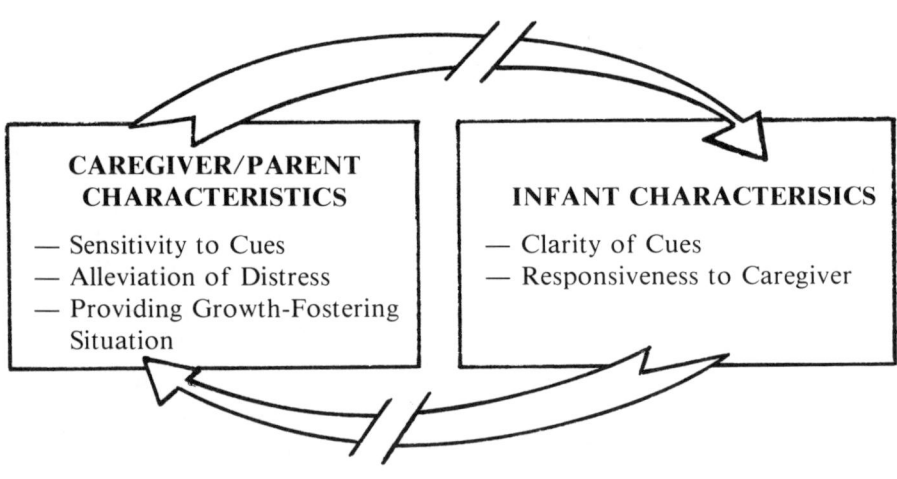

Figure 2. The Barnard model.

To facilitate the patterns of parent-infant interaction conceptualized in Figure 2, the coach reviews infant states of consciousness with parents so that they understand the messages that are being communicated. For example, infants in light sleep may smile, have brief fussy periods, or make crying sounds. Some parents may interpret these signals as hunger or as a waking state and attempt to feed or arouse the child before he or she is ready. The perinatal coach also demonstrates habituation in the infant and a wide variety of comforting techniques. The coach points out infant behavior such as lip grimace, diffuse body movements, gaze aversion, and crying, which may indicate distress and the infants' attempts to comfort themselves. Common comforting actions include hand-to-mouth movements, sucking fingers or fist, alerting to voices or faces, and changing position. Parents are taught how to comfort the infant through visual stimulation, soothing verbal stimuli, touch, rocking, position change, and swaddling, so that their reactions to a distressed infant go beyond picking it up or feeding it.

In addition, the coach demonstrates the infant's ability to react in a sophisticated way to the environment by selectively responding to stimuli. Parents are often impressed by this level of infant competence. The coach will also identify those infants who may have more difficulty with this task and act as an interpreter and guide until the parents understand and use interactional skills. This type of coaching is viewed as a collaborative, supportive effort.

Target Populations

As a primary prevention measure, a perinatal coach should be made available for all first-time parents, according to Hoover. This skills training provides intervention for all new parents before any particular problem has been identified. Because anticipated and new parenthood are difficult and stressful periods for all parents, there seems to be no logical reason to restrict services to high-risk families. Another reason for not limiting the program is that, at this point, there are no clearcut guidelines for reliably targeting who is at risk and who is not.

However, some adults are obviously at higher risk than others for having difficulty interacting with newborns, and these populations may require special attention. These groups include: (1) those adults who have a child later in life; (2) those adults with certain restrictive cultural traditions; and (3) those adults who were reared in an abnormal environment.

Delayed Parenthood. Hoover believes that those adults who choose to have their first child later in life "need to refresh their memory about what it is like to be a child." Since adults communicate primarily through verbal behaviors and cognitive modes, they must relearn and practice skills they have forgotten. This will allow them to adapt to the interactional model presented in Figure 2. The relearning and use of sensory skills is easier for older parents if they are given the opportunity to practice with the assistance of a trained perinatal coach.

> Mrs. B. is a 32-year-old woman who has just delivered her first child, a son. She is a successful business executive who has learned to "turn off" her emotions in order to promote her career. When given her son shortly after birth and told to "get acquainted" with him, Mrs. B. responded, "How can I get to know him when he doesn't even talk?" Mr. and Mrs. B. responded well to the perinatal coach and became involved in their lessons as if they were college courses with a final examination. They were fascinated with the social capability of their infant and with their own newfound abilities to communicate with him.

Parents with Restricting Cultural Traditions. Some men do not believe that it is "manly" to express oneself to an infant. Others believe that infants do not have the ability to communicate or that an infant will be spoiled if given too much attention. Some cultures recommend the isolation of mothers and infants for a period of time or restriction of the infant's movements with swaddling. The perinatal coach demonstrates for parents the abilities that are present in the infant, and allows the family to assimilate this into their own cultural beliefs. The coach encourages the parents to interact with their infant. In general, these parents are excited and surprised by what their infants can do.

> Mr. C. is a 20-year-old factory worker. His response to an explanation of perinatal coaching was, "That's my wife's job. I do not need to know anything about the baby. You are not going to catch me making goo-goo faces." After the coaching experience, however, Mr. C. could not wait to "show the guys" what he could do and how smart his son was.

Parents Who Experienced a Negative Early Childhood. A childhood devoid of positive interpersonal relationships and joys most likely did not teach helpful interpersonal skills. In fact, sensory input may be associated with unpleasant experiences—for example, touch hurts, verbal stimuli are derogatory, and eye contact is established only in fits of anger. Such adults need to be shown how to use their senses in a positive way and how to interpret their infant's messages. The perinatal coach provides immediate positive feedback to these parents to increase their confidence. In extreme cases, long-term professional involvement must also be available.

Organizing a Perinatal Program

A perinatal coaching program can be started within a variety of organizational settings, including a physician's office, hospital, local health department, community mental health office, counseling service, or university. The lead agency must have access to families prenatally, be able to initiate visits in the hospital and the home, and take responsibility for coordinating the program and supervising the coaches. Because a perinatal coaching program cannot function in isolation from other professionals and services, community support must be obtained and community-wide linkages established. A coordinator is needed to administer the program and act as a liaison.

The coaches may be volunteers recruited from the membership of civic organizations. Approximately 80 coaches per year would be required to service 300 families. The basic coaching process with one family would require about eight hours of the coach's time. Evaluation of the program and its methods is needed and has not yet been undertaken.

SUMMARY COMMENTS

Robert A. Hoekelman, M.D.

The major objectives of this conference have been to define normal parenting, to define problem parenting, to review the research in these areas, and to offer recommendations concerning child health professionals intervening effectively once high-risk parenting has been identified. These problems have been approached from a variety of perspectives by individuals from many disciplines. This conference includes one demographer/sociologist, one economist, one educator, five nurses, one social worker, three pediatricians, one obstetrician/gynecologist, four psychologists, and three psychiatrists.

The questions of who needs intervention, who intervenes, how much it will cost, who is going to pay for it, and whether or not it will be effective, need to be answered. We have been able to identify the parents and children who are at risk. They key risk factors were summarized masterfully by Henry Ricciuti in his multifactor model in which he pointed out the characteristics of the molar environment, of the family, of the mother and her prenatal and perinatal condition, and of the individual child, all of which may lead to either good or bad parenting but which can and do lead to adverse outcomes, for the parents, the child, and society.

One particular concern is the establishment of a vicious cycle, as seen in the battered-child situation. We know that a battered child may become a battering parent. This may be true of all of the social ills we have discussed. Certainly, the costs in terms of human suffering and expenditures of health and social resources are extremely high. The prevalence of these high-risk circumstances is enormous. In fact, some risk factors in parenting probably exist in all of us; being a parent for the first time is stressful in itself. The cost of providing interventions for all of these adults and children at risk will be extremely high, so we must examine their effectiveness carefully.

Historically, we have been extremely successful in bringing maternal and child health in this country from the abysmally poor levels of a century ago to the highest levels we have ever known. We can currently boast of the lowest maternal and infant death rates, the lowest incidence of childhood infectious and nutritional diseases, the lowest hospitalization rates for children, and the most equitable distribution of maternal and child health-care services ever recorded in this country. It would seem logical, then, that we could now turn our energies and resources to reducing, preventing, and managing the problems of high-risk parenting identified at this conference. This, however, may not be easy. Certain professional and political decisions will profoundly affect our ability to intervene.

Pediatricians have always been interested in the prevention of physical and emotional illness and have spent much time in this pursuit. We have provided immunizations and child-health supervision at regularly scheduled visits to identify problems early on and provide anticipatory guidance in child-rearing. In the late 1960s, and again in the early 1970s, the American Academy of Pediatrics established recommendations on the frequency with which well children, from infancy through childhood and adolescence, should be seen by their pediatricians for these purposes. The recommendations were based on opinion. There were no data to show that these visits made any difference in terms of improving the physical and emotional health of children. It is disturbing to me that the Academy of Pediatrics is now proposing new recommendations that increase by almost 50 percent the visits that children should make to their pediatricians from birth through adolescence. This is disturbing because even the currently recommended well-child schedule is not supported by scientific evidence, and in adhering to a schedule requiring so many visits (20 during the first 21 years of life), pediatricians will have time for little else and will be able to provide care for fewer children.

The average well-child visit to the pediatrican lasts 10 minutes, during which time the pediatrican devotes 52 seconds to anticipatory guidance. For adolescents, the average time pediatricians spend in providing guidance is seven seconds. You cannot do very much during that length of time; in fact, you can hardly ask a question. That is an average figure, to be sure, but it means that in most visits, there is no discussion at all with adolescents concerning how they feel about themselves, their parents, their peers, their sexuality, or their other concerns. Guidance and direction in these matters are not provided. In my view, a schedule that calls for fewer, but longer, well-child visits for only those in whom a need is indicated would be more effective in dealing with the issues that contribute to high-risk parenting.

It is time that we examine how all of our health and social professionals, not just pediatricians, spend their time. We must determine if there are tasks they now do that could be performed by others, that could be performed less often, or that do not need to be performed at all. If it can be shown that any of these alternatives to the use of valuable and scarce professional time can be implemented without decreasing the quality of care to unacceptable levels, we will be able to devote the time saved to preventing and managing the outcomes of high-risk parenting.

The current political climate at the federal level and most state levels is not supportive of the kinds of intervention we have discussed. Politicians do not often buy the concept that prevention of a problem now will save money later. They are interested in balancing this year's budget, not in saving money for the budgets of the next administration.

Within the past year, deep cuts have been made in federal programs that were developed to improve maternal and child health over the past 20 years. If unstemmed, federal spending cutbacks will relinquish wholly to the states 43 programs that provide, among other things, support for pregnant women and adolescents, child-health supervision, prevention of childhood diseases, treatment of handicapped children, training of primary care physicians and nurses, prevention and treatment of alcohol and drug abuse and mental illness, family planning, migrant health centers, nutrition programs for women, infants, and children (WIC), adoption assistance, foster care, management of child abuse, food stamps, and aid to families with dependent children. Most state governors and legislators have already indicated that their states will not be able to support any of these programs at their current levels of federal funding. For some, no monies will be provided at all. Several federal laws now under consideration, if passed, will outlaw abortions and the use of our most effective contraceptives (the IUD and the pill) and will require that parents be informed of any contraceptive information given to their adolescent children through federally funded family-planning programs.

Such federal and state spending policies and conservative antiabortion and anticontraceptive initiatives will, without question, markedly increase maternal and neonatal mortality and morbidity and will reverse most of the gains we have made in the last generation in improving the physical and social well-being of mothers and children.

It is therefore difficult, in light of these professional and political considerations, to be optimistic about our prospects for minimizing high-risk parenting using the methods described at this conference or any others we may devise. Indeed, we will have all we can do to keep the problems of high-risk parenting at their current disastrous levels. Nevertheless, we must continue to find better ways to deal with these problems and, working both within and beyond our professional bounds—that is, in the political arena—reverse the tides that threaten to wash away the gains we have made in preventing and managing poor parenting outcomes.

APPENDIX

FUNDING FOR AND COST-BENEFIT ANALYSIS OF SERVICES FOR HIGH-RISK FAMILIES AND INFANTS

Nancy T. Greenspan, M.A.

Families with multiple risk factors, such as psychological impairment in the parents and compromised coping abilities in the infants, require a wide range of health and support services to rear relatively healthy children. Funding for the provision of these services to the parents and children is often provided under federal programs administered by the states, with funds usually allocated on a local basis. The major federal health and welfare programs are: Medicaid (Title XIX), Social Services (Title XX), Maternal and Child Health (Title V), and Community Mental Health Centers. Although the legislated scope of these programs covers most of those services needed by high-risk families and infants, such factors as insufficient funding levels, lack of integration of services, and the challenges and barriers for this population group in using available services usually lead to inadequate levels of care.

For example, under Medicaid, a state-administered medical assistance program, each state has some flexibility in defining who is eligible for Medicaid and what services are covered. Although federal regulation mandates that states cover all individuals who receive cash assistance under Aid to Families with Dependent Children (AFDC) and most individuals who receive cash assistance under Supplemental Security Income (SSI) for aged, blind, and disabled, at its option a state may include financially eligible pregnant women, families where the father is unemployed, and children of two-parent families who meet the AFDC income standard. At the present time only 16 states actually provide Medicaid services to children in intact families. The Select Panel for the Promotion of Child Health found that these eligibility criteria cover only about half of the poor children in the country and that in six states less than 30% of all poor children are covered.

Approximately 16 percent of the Medicaid budget is spent on services for persons aged 21 or younger. These funds cover certain basic services such as hospitalization, physician, laboratory and x-ray services, family planning, and for persons under 21, early and periodic screening, diagnosis, and treatment. In some cases home health-care services and transportation are available. However, because the states have discretion over the level of payment to many kinds of providers as well as the number of visits allowed, those eligible often have difficulty finding and receiving appropriate care.

In July 1981, Congress passed the Omnibus Reconciliation Act of 1981, which requires that many of the above programs either be incorporated into block grants to the states or be amended to grant the states greater flexibility in the disposition of funds. For example, Title XX of the Social Security Act, which provides grants to states for social and support services to low- and moderate-income families, has been amended so that states now determine eligibility standards and the types of services to be provided. Under the new block grant for Maternal and Child Health Services, the states have greater discretion over apportionment of funds and are not required to target funds for certain project areas. Because of these changes, funding programs are and will be in a state of flux.

The inadequacy of the government programs has led child-health professionals to establish private, nonprofit programs that perform outreach, offer special services to the parents and infants, and help coordinate local public health and welfare services. Accompanying these programs has been an interest in the allocation of specific funds for them by local or state governments. However, in these times of fiscal restraint, policy makers are even more cautious than usual about funding a program without the certainty of significant social and cost benefits.

As an initial step in providing information to policy makers, Greenspan has calculated cost-effectiveness benefits for two cases from a high-risk parenting intervention program in Prince Georges County, Maryland—The Clinical Infant Development Program. Both cases received preventive services for approximately three years.

In each case, the primary patient was a newborn infant, with services also rendered to the parents and other siblings.

The basic methodology for the cost-effectiveness study follows the usual calculation for the cost of the services but then deviates from the approach in determining benefits. Because of the lack of long-term outcome data (the program is only five years old), Greenspan hypothesized five different possible scenarios resulting after intervention. They ranged from a worst case of almost total dependence on government support to the best case of being totally self-supporting and requiring no intervention services. Probabilities of the likelihood of each scenario occurring with and without intervention were then attached to each. Cost differences were determined and net expected benefits derived for each case.

The expected net benefit and cost-benefit ratio findings from these two cases strongly suggest that early intervention for high-risk infants is very cost-effective. Depending on the case, the results show a savings to society of between $93,000 and $145,000 in present value terms (1981). This means that the actual dollar amounts saved in the future are considerably higher, but because money in the future is valued less than in the present, it is necessary to deduct part of the future savings, like a choice of being offered $250,000 in 18 years or the present day equivalent of $150,000. The cost-benefit ratios for the five scenarios range from 1:5 to 1:7.

In addition, it should be noted that it is quite possible to have much higher social costs than those enumerated in the five scenarios. Should any hypothesized scenario contain serious social problems such as robbery, homicide, or drug abuse, costs escalate quickly. For instance, it has been estimated that by curing a heroin addict, the present value of the benefit to society of uncommitted thefts due to heroin addiction is $332,000. When added to the $56,000 benefit to society from future earnings, the total benefit is $388,000. Calculations show that including heroin addiction in one scenario increases the average expected net benefit by 72 percent, showing how conservative the above estimates are. Court and correctional facility costs for serious crimes are even greater, especially when considering the harm to the victim. In 1981, the construction costs alone of a maximum security cell in a federal prison has been estimated at $75,000.

Although the above approach needs to be replicated for additional cases in the Clinical Infant Intervention Program to determine if they are representative of the program as a whole, the findings for the two cases are consistent and indicate a positive social value to the interventions undertaken.

BIBLIOGRAPHY

Adelson E, Blos P Jr: *A Demographic Examination of an Infant Mental Health Clinical Research Population.* Washington, DC, National Institute of Mental Health, publication no. 24746

Ainsworth M, Bell SM, Stayton D: Infant-mother attachment and social development: socialization as a product of reciprocal responsiveness to signals. In *The Integration of the Child into a Social World.* Edited by Richards M. Cambridge, England, Cambridge University Press, 1974, pp 99–135

Aradine CR: Development of Toddlers with Long-Term Tracheostomies. Ann Arbor, University of Michigan, unpublished doctoral dissertation, 1978

Aradine C: Home care of young children with long-term tracheostomies. *Am J Maternal-Child Nurs* 5:121–125, 1980

Aradine C, Uman H, Shapiro V: Collaborative treatment of a sick premature and his parents. *Issues Comprehen Pediatr Nurs* 3:29–41, 1978

Baldwin W, Cain V: The children of teenage parents. *Fam Plann Perspect* 12:34–43, 1980

Benfield DG, Leib S, Vollman J: Grief response of parents to neonatal death and parent participation in deciding care. *Pediatrics* 62:171–177, 1978

Report of the Select Panel for the Promotion of Child Health to the United States Congress and the Secretary of Health and Human Services: *Better Health for Our Children: A National Strategy,* vol I-III. Washington DC, US Government Printing Office, 1980

Boisvart MJ: The battered child syndrome. *Social Casework* 53:475–480, 1972

Briggs E: Transition to parenthood. *Maternal-Child Nurs J* 8:69–83, 1979

Bronfenbrenner U: *The Ecology of Human Development: Experiments by Nature and Design.* Cambridge, Harvard University Press, 1979

Chamberlin R, Olds D: Improving the Delivery of Preventive Services to Mothers and Children. Conference sponsored by the American Academy of Pediatrics, Washington DC, June 15–17, 1980

Chess S: Developmental theory revisited. *Can J Psychiatry* 24:101–112, 1979

Chess S, Thomas A, Birch H: Characteristics of the individual child's behavioral responses to the environment. *Am J Orthopsychiatry* 29:791–802, 1959

Chess S, Thomas A, Birch HG: *Your Child is a Person*. New York, Viking, 1965

Children's Defense Fund: Preliminary Findings of a Study of the Use of Medicaid for Child/Adolescent Mental Health Services. August 1981

Coddington MN: A mother struggles to cope with her child's deteriorating illness. *Maternal-Child Nurs J* 5:39–44, 1976

Comer J: *School Power: Implications of An Intervention Project*, New York, Free Press, 1980

Comer J, Poussaint A: *Black Child Care*. New York, Simon and Schuster, 1975

Cowan CP, Cowan PA, Coie L, et al: Becoming a family: the impact of a first child's birth on the couple's relationship. In *The First Child and Family Formation*. Edited by Miller W, Newman L. Chapel Hill, University of North Carolina Press, 1978

Erickson MT: The influence of health factors on psychological variables predicting complications of pregnancy, labor and delivery. *Psychosomatic Res* 20:21–24, 1976

Fraiberg S, Fraiberg L (eds): *Clinical Studies in Infant Mental Health: The First Year of Life*. New York, Basic Books, 1980

Fraiberg S: Intervention and Outcome in an Infant Psychiatry Program. Final Report, Mental Health contract no. 24746, January 1981

Field TM: Interactions of pre-term and term infants with their lower- and middle-class teenage and adult mothers. In *High-Risk Infants and Children*. Edited by Field TM, et al. New York, Academic Press, 1980

Field TM, Widmayer SM, Stringer S, et al: Teenage, lower-class, black mothers and their preterm infants: an intervention and developmental follow-up. *Child Dev* 51:426–436, 1980

Gil DF: *Violence against Children*. Cambridge, Harvard University Press, 1970

Goldfogel L: Working with the parent of a dying child. *Am J Nurs* 70:1674–1679, 1970

Greenspan SI: Intelligence and adaptation: an integration of psychoanalytic and piagetian developmental psychology. In *Psychology Issues,* monograph no. 47/48. New York, International Universities Press, 1979

Greenspan SI: *Psychopathology and Adaptation in Infancy and Early Childhood: Principles of Clinical Diagnosis and Preventive Intervention.* New York, International Universities Press, 1981

Greenspan SI, Lourie RS: Developmental structuralist approach to the classification of adaptive and pathologic personality organizations: infancy and early childhood. *Am J Psychiatry* 138:725-735, 1981

Greenspan S, Pollack GH (eds): *Infancy and Early Childhood,* vol 1. Washington DC, National Institute of Mental Health, 1980

HDS Transportation Initiative: A Report on Research Findings. Washington DC, Office of Human Development Services, DHHS, January 1981

Helfer RE: Perinatal coaching guide. *Pediatr Basics* 26:10-14, 1980

Hollingsworth D, Kotchen J: Gynecologic age and its relation to neonatal outcome. In *Pregnancy and Childbearing during Adolescence: Research Priorities for the 1980's.* Edited by McAnarney ER, Stickle G. New York, Alan R. Liss. In press, 1982

Hunter RS, Kilstrom N, Kraybill EN, et al: Antecedents of child abuse and neglect in premature infants: a prospective study in a newborn intensive care unit. *Pediatrics* 61:629-635, 1978

Johnson D, Maitland E: *Lucy: The Beginnings of Human Kind.* New York, Simon and Schuster, 1981

Johnson SH: Avoiding communication blocks with high risk parents. *Issues Comprehen Pediatr Nurs* 5:61, 1980

Johnson SH: *High Risk Parenting.* Philadelphia, JB Lippincott, 1979

Johnson SH: Interaction deprivation of the mother with transported premature infant. *J Nurse-Midwifery* 30: 1981

Kempe CH, Silverman FN, Steele BF, et al: The battered-child syndrome. *JAMA* 181:17-24, 1962

Kennell JH, Klaus MH: Caring for parents of an infant who dies. In *Maternal Infant Bonding.* Edited by Klaus JH, Kennel MH. St. Louis, CV Mosby, 1976, pp 209-239

Kent JT: Follow-up study of abused children. *J Pediatr Psychol* 4:25-31, 1976

Kohlberg L: Stage and sequence: the cognitive-developmental approach to socialization. In *Handbook of Socialization Theory and Research*. Edited by Goslin D. Chicago, Rand McNally, 1969

Larson C: Efficacy of prenatal and postpartum home visitis on child health and development. *Pediatrics* 66:191-197, 1980

Leal CA: Treatment of abused and neglected pre-school children in a city hospital. *Child Psychiatry Soc Issues Psychiatric Ann* 6:5, 1976

Mahler MD, Pine F, Bergman A: *The Psychological Birth of the Human Infant*. New York, Basic Books, 1975

McAnarney E, Lawrence R, Aten M, et al: Discrimination of the age of the adolescent females on the basis of facial cues. *Adoles Health Care* 1:213-216, 1981

McKeever PT: Fathering the chronically ill child. *Am J Maternal-Child Nurs* 6:124-128, 1981

Miller H, Merritt T: *Fetal Growth in Humans*. Chicago, Year Book, 1979

Moore K, Hofferth S, Wertheimer R, et al: Teenage childbearing: consequences for women, families and government welfare expenditures. In *Teenage Parents and Their Offspring*. Edited by Scott K, Field T, Robertson E. New York, Grune and Stratton, 1981, pp. 35-55

Newberger CM: The cognitive structure of parenthood: designing a descriptive measure. *N Direct Child* 1:45-67, 1980

Newberger C: Parental Conceptions of Children and Childrearing: A Structural-Developmental Analysis. Cambridge, Harvard University, unpublished doctoral dissertation, 1977

O'Connor S, Vietze PM, Sherrod KB: et al: Reduced incidence of parenting inadequacy following rooming-in. *Pediatrics* 66:176-182, 1980

Olds D: The experimental ecology of pregnancy, birth and early childrearing among families at risk. Paper prepared for the Conference on Research Perspectives in the Ecology of Human Development, Ithaca, Cornell University, August 1977

Olds D: Improving formal services for mothers and children. In *Protecting Children from Abuse and Neglect: Creating and Maintaining Family Support Systems*. Edited by Garbarino J, Stocking H. San Francisco, Jossey-Bass, 1980

Osofsky HJ: Expectant and new fatherhood as a developmental crisis. *Bull Menninger Clin*. In press, 1981

Osofsky HJ, Osofsky JD: Normal adaptation to pregnancy and new parenthood. In *Parent-Infant Relationships.* Edited by Taylor, PM. New York, Grune and Stratton, 1980

Parens H: Parenthood as a developmental phase. *J Am Psychoanal Assoc* 23:154-165, 1975

Piaget J: *The Moral Judgment of the Child.* New York, Harcourt Press, 1950

Polansky NA, et al: *Damaged Parents: An Anatomy of Child Nelect.* Chicago, University of Chicago Press, 1981

Rees WD: The bereaved and their hallucinations. In *Bereavement: Its Psychosocial Aspects.* Edited by Shoenberg B, Gerber I, Wiener A, et al. New York, Columbia University Press, 1975, pp 66-71

Reports of the National Juvenile Justice Assessment Centers: *A National Assessment of Serious Juvenile Crime and the Juvenile Justice System: The Need for a Rational Response,* vol IV. Washington DC, US Department of Justice, April 1980

Ricciuti HN: Adverse social and biological influences on early development. In *Ecological Factors in Human Development.* Edited by McGurk H. Amsterdam, North-Holland Press, 1977

Riesch S: Enhancement of mother-infant social interaction. *J Obstet Gynecol Nurs* July/August: 242-246, 1979

Rothenberg P, Varga P: The relationship between age of mother and development. *Am J Pub Health* 71:810-817, 1981

Rutter M: *Maternal Deprivation Reassessed,* 2nd ed. Middlesex, Penguin Books, 1981

Selman R: *The Growth of Interpersonal Understanding: Developmental and Clinical Analyses.* New York, Academic Press, 1980

Slade CI: Working with the parents of high risk newborns. *J Obstet Gynecol Nurs* 6:21-26, 1977

Spinetta JJ, Rigler D: The child-abusing parent: psychological review. *Psychol Bull* 77:296-304, 1972

Statistical Abstract of the United States, 1980. US Department of Commerce, Washington DC, US Government Printing Office, 1980

Tavorima JB, et al: Psychosocial effects on parents of raising a physically handicapped child. *Abnor Child Psychol* 9:212-231, 1980

Thomas A, Chess S: *Temperament and Development.* New York, Brunner/Mazel, 1977

Thomas A, Sillen S: *Racism and Psychiatry.* New York, Brunner/Mazel, 1972

Whaley P: Relieving parental anxiety. *J Obstet Gynecol Nurs* 8:49–55, 1979

Johnson & Johnson

Baby Products Company
Grandview Road
Skillman, NJ 08558

1-800/526-3967 (outside NJ)
800/942-7764 (NJ only)